Sharing the Word

Preaching in the Roundtable Church

Sharing the Word

Lucy Atkinson Rose

Westminster John Knox Press
Louisville, Kentucky

Scripture quotations from the New Revised Standard Version
of the Bible are copyright ©1989 by the Division of Christian Education
of the National Council of the Churches of Christ in the U.S.A.
and are used by permission.

Portions of the Introduction were previously published as
"Conversational Preaching: A Proposal,"
Journal for Preachers (Advent 1995): 26–30.

Book design by Jennifer K. Cox
Cover design by Kevin Darst
Cover illustration courtesy of Project Salvador

First edition
Published by Westminster John Knox Press
Louisville, Kentucky

This book is printed on acid-free paper that meets the
American National Standards Institute Z39.48 standard. ∞

PRINTED IN THE UNITED STATES OF AMERICA
00 01 02 03 04 05 06 — 10 9 8 7 6 5 4 3 2

Library of Congress Cataloging-in-Publication Data

Rose, Lucy Atkinson, date.
    Sharing the word : preaching in the roundtable church / Lucy
Atkinson Rose. —1st ed.
        p.   cm.
    Includes bibliographical references and index.
    ISBN 0-664-25658-9 (alk. paper)
    1. Preaching. I. Title.
BV4211.R67 1996
251—dc21   96-49122

Contents

Foreword

Lucy Rose is the last person who would tell you how to read her book. She might be willing, however, for me to suggest a way to begin. Even though her subject is preaching, her *real* subject is the church. One begins, therefore, not with the pulpit but with the church. Moreover, Lucy's image of the church is not row upon row of pews facing an elevated leader of word and sacrament. Neither is it the "remove the pulpit and pews and sit on the floor" rebellion of the 1960s. Rather, her image is that of a table around which are gathered the listeners, the seekers, those longing for God and for one another. Together they search the Scriptures and share their responses to God's love extended in Christ and in the community that still prays, "Lord, we believe; help our unbelief." Around the table are those still listening for an authoritative voice to relieve them of the responsibility for their own faith, those weary of the old jargon who are turning to poets and tellers of stories for a fresh word, those who are still on the porch of the church and nervous about coming inside, those who have been there since day one but who can no longer remember why, and those who reverence Scripture and things sacred but who fear investigation. Some are accustomed to being listened to; others, long silent, are surprised and empowered by the sound of their own voices.

Among these sits the preacher, but which one is it? A visitor arriving late might not know immediately, since the lively conversation involves many. The image does raise an important question: Is Lucy thereby diminishing preaching? By no means! It could be argued that she is in fact enlarging it, for she presents preaching as the work of the whole church.

Nevertheless, some preachers and homileticians may grow uncomfortable and leave the table early. No one would understand their action more than Lucy who, by reason of training and tradition, carries within herself all the older images of preaching, and not without appreciation. She listens to all the major voices in homiletical theory—from John Broadus to the present—with acknowledged indebtedness. In fact, insights from the past figure prominently in her move into a future unrealized and in many ways unknown. It is not as though Lucy is entertaining a notion about preaching that is without genealogy, having neither mother nor father. Her principal quarrel (it hardly seems a quarrel, she is so gracious) with homileticians past and present is that they fail to see or are afraid to carry through the implications for preaching that are present in their own theories and theologies. Lucy is willing to press forward with these insights from practitioners and theorists, both inside and outside the sanctuary, and having done so, she is now willing to listen to any and all responses. All she asks of us is the hospitality of our minds.

Lucy means it when she says preaching is a conversation. If she can keep alive a conversation that often ends too soon, she will be pleased, and all of us will be blessed.

Fred B. Craddock

Preface

This book describes a communal, heuristic, and nonhierarchical understanding of preaching. It is a probe, an effort to put into words what I and others hope for when we preach and when we listen to sermons.

For twenty-five years I have preached and read what others claim about preaching, and until recently I have not been able to put the two together. If what I do is preaching, it is not reflected in the literature that describes and defines preaching. And if what I read about preaching is true, then what I do is not really preaching. My refusal to give up either preaching or reflection on preaching has led me to an understanding of preaching that I call "conversational."

My hope is that this conversational description of preaching will join other descriptions of the whys, whats, and hows of preaching. My aim is not to narrow the field of homiletics around my proposal. Instead, by describing the contours of an additional understanding of preaching, I seek to enrich homiletics as a collection of differing interpretations about the preaching enterprise.

The journey that is taken in this book has at times been lonely and scary, for I am painfully aware that my descriptions of preaching run counter to the powerful currents in homiletical thinking. I would like to acknowledge my gratitude to God for some of those who have helped me preach and think about preaching, as well as those who have supported me on this journey.

First, I am deeply thankful for Fred B. Craddock, my mentor and the director of my dissertation on which this book is based. With graciousness and wisdom he encouraged me to "think [my] own thoughts" (1974, 157) and claim my God-given gifts.

A second homiletical mentor for whom I am grateful is Eugene L. Lowry. I remain firmly grounded in his narrative understanding of preaching and value the conversations that have arisen from our friendship.

Other friends and colleagues in the Academy of Homiletics have encouraged and sharpened my insights as a preacher and scholar. Among them are many of the scholars whom I discuss in chapter 3. I will value our ongoing conversations about homiletical theory. I am especially indebted to Edwina Hunter and Joan Delaplane, the "mothers" of us second-generation women homileticians, and to my friend and homiletical compatriot, Jana Childers.

Four books that sought to reconstruct homiletical theory became my particular companions on my journey. The authors are Robert E. C. Browne (1958), Christine M. Smith (1989), Joseph Sittler (1966), and George W. Swank (1981).

Other scholars for whom I am grateful belong outside the field of homiletics. Years ago I found myself at-home in the world of Christian feminist scholarship. Here Letty M. Russell, Phyllis Trible, Rosemary Radford Ruether, and Elisabeth Schüssler Fiorenza nurtured my growing conviction that my experiences as a woman are a legitimate and inescapable dimension of all that I am and do.

More recently I have found myself at-home in the world of postmodern scholarship with its multiple, often conflicting, voices. Here there is room at last for my alternative voice. Here I am also discomforted as I continue to recognize, lament, and risk—slowly, reluctantly, and yet gratefully—my blinders as a Euro-American, middle-class, educated, employed woman.

I am equally grateful for those local congregations where I preached and worshiped Sunday after Sunday and learned about life lived together as the people of God. Prior to my ordination in 1975 in the former Southern Presbyterian Church and during the following eight years, I served several Presbyterian churches in North Carolina. I thank God for the John Calvin Church, Salisbury; the Summerville Church, Lillington; the First Church, Sanford; the First Church, Rocky Mount; and the Bethesda Church, Aberdeen. Currently, the worshiping communities of Clifton Presbyterian Church, Atlanta, Georgia, and the Community of Hospitality, Decatur, Georgia, have honed my convictions about preaching.

Since 1983, my colleagues at Columbia Theological Seminary, both faculty and students, have been supportive of me personally and interested in my emerging insights into the enterprise of preaching. They have been my sounding boards and my collaborators. Particularly I am grateful for my co-workers in the area of preaching, Wade P. Huie and Charles L. Campbell.

Finally, I offer my heartfelt thanks to God for my parents and family. My parents are still my beloved mentors: my father, Ben Lacy Rose; and my mother, Anne Thompson Rose. They both nurtured me in a biblical, church-centered, spiritual faith. My mother gave me space and encouragement to grow as a unique child of God from the day I was born until today; my father engaged me in many discussions of faith and preaching. I have followed in my father's footsteps as a pastor and teacher of preaching; I have followed in my mother's footsteps in my efforts to provide hospitable space and to celebrate the gifts of others.

I thank God also for my husband Gerry Cook, my daughter Lucy Mac Cook, as well as Dean Shirley and Louie Dowis, members of our household. I am grateful for their willingness to let me sit for hours at the computer, for their fixing meals and bringing me popcorn, for their suggestions that I take breaks, and for their reminders of the larger world in which discipleship must be lived out. In particular I could not have made the journey thus far without my husband. As an excellent, though unconventional, sermon critic and lay theologian, as well as the provider of safe space for my hurts and fears, my joyful discoveries, and my weariness, he has been my intellectual and emotional partner during the entire journey that has found a resting-place in this book.

Acknowledgments

Grateful acknowledgment is made to the following publishers and copyright holders for permission to reprint excerpts from the following:

Margaret Atwood, "It is Dangerous to Read Newspapers," in *Selected Poems 1966–1984,* copyright © Margaret Atwood 1990. Reprinted by permission of Oxford University Press Canada.

Lynn Emanuel, "Silence. She Is Six Years Old," in *The Dig and Hotel Fiesta,* copyright ©1994 by Lynn Emanuel. Used with the permission of the author and of the University of Illinois Press.

Jane Flanders, "The House That Fear Built: Warsaw, 1943," in *Timepiece,* by Jane Flanders, copyright ©1988. Reprinted by permission of the University of Pittsburgh Press.

Maxine Kumin, excerpt from *A Way of Staying Sane,* by Maxine Kumin, copyright © by Maxine Kumin. Reprinted by permission of the author and of Curtis Brown, Ltd.

Julian of Norwich, excerpt from *Meditations with Julian of Norwich,* edited by Brendon Doyle, copyright 1983. Reprinted by permission of Bear and Company, Inc., P.O. Drawer 2860, Santa Fe, NM 87504.

Dorothee Soelle, excerpt from *Revolutionary Patience,* translated by Rita Kimber and Robert Kimber, copyright ©1977. Used by permission of Orbis Books, Maryknoll, NY.

Introduction

For years I have been painfully aware that existing homiletical theories about the whys, whats, and hows of preaching do not describe my expectations when I preach, when I listen to sermons on Sunday mornings, and when I try to help some students develop their gifts for preaching. In addition, conversations with students and pastors have convinced me that I am not alone in my yearning for additional insights into the ecclesial practice called preaching. If homiletics is, at least in part, reflection on the actual practices of preaching, then many of us do not find within the homiletical literature reflection that takes seriously our experiences of preaching. Aware of my discomfort with the current state of homiletics, I set out on a journey to discover the missing pieces.

This book reflects, first, my listening and responding to the theories I have discerned in contemporary homiletical literature and, second, my suggestions for an additional understanding of preaching that is communal, heuristic, and nonhierarchical.[1]

A Personal Crisis

My journey that resulted in this book began with a crisis. In the spring of 1990, after eight years of parish ministry, both as an associate and as a solo pastor, and after seven years of teaching preaching at a seminary, I realized I could not articulate a coherent theory of preaching. My dilemma came into clear focus following a student's evaluation of her Introduction to Preaching course. She thanked my colleague and me for teaching her how to preach and then added, "But the question never asked or answered was, Why do we preach?" With distressing clarity I realized I was not sure how I would answer that question. I began to wonder, What *is* the purpose of preaching? What is preaching's function in the life of the church? What are my and my students' roles as preachers? What is the congregation's role? What do I believe about preaching? And is there a single answer to any of these questions?

These questions did not emerge because I was unfamiliar with preaching. My relationship to preaching began during my childhood when I heard my father preach good sermons Sunday after Sunday. I grew up *listening* to his sermons because my parents promised us four children a nickel up to a quarter for every point or illustration we could remember and relate at the Sunday dinner table. Very quickly I discovered that if I remembered five parts of the sermon, I could always earn a dime, quite a treasure in my mind in the early 1950s. My arithmetic went like this: "The first person to 'go' is my younger brother. He sometimes remembers the most obvious story—one down. Then it's my turn—two. Next are my two older sisters' turns, and if their contributions are ones I have remembered, there go my three and four. Then it's back to my brother, who never has a second contribution. So it's my turn again, and I can describe my fifth point or story—my second contribution—and get my dime." And I remember the excitement of a further realization, "If my brother and sisters don't listen to the sermon, I *could* get a quarter!" I therefore began to listen very attentively to each sermon and usually to all of the sermon in order to identify and remember five points or stories. Even today I can almost recapture the thrill of this Sunday ritual. I can almost conjure up the fun of earning at least a dime and hearing my parents' exclamations of surprise and delight.

During my teenage years my relationship to preaching deepened. My listening to sermons evolved into my evaluating sermons. The summer before I entered fifth grade, my father began to teach preaching at Union Theological Seminary in Richmond, Virginia. No longer preaching regularly in the same church, he was often the guest preacher in nearby and distant churches. Many times I accompanied him, and many times he and I discussed the sermon on the way home. Listening to and evaluating sermons is in my bones. I was therefore surprised when my questions about preaching rose to the surface in 1990.

If preaching is in my bones, theories about preaching have for a long time been in my head. My questions about preaching did not arise out of my unfamiliarity with homiletical theory. At Union Theological Seminary, Virginia, as a student and at Columbia Theological Seminary as a teacher of preaching, I read widely and deeply in homiletical theory. What is preaching all about? In 1990 I could quote others' answers. But I did not have an answer that resonated with my own deepest beliefs or experiences of preaching. Something was missing.

Returning to Basics:
Relistening, Rethinking

Out of this crisis arose my decision to revisit those scholars who in recent years have articulated the fundamental issues of homiletics: preaching's purpose and content, as well as such technical elements as sermonic language and form. As I explored again the homiletical literature, I initially wanted to identify my colleagues in the field of homiletics who were already saying what I was beginning to articulate about preaching. I knew that I gravitated to those developments in homiletical theory that have broadened and enriched the field beyond what might be termed preaching's traditional or classical theory. I searched for what was new and marginal because previous explorations had failed to reflect adequately my experiences of preaching. At the same time, the theories I continued to encounter as dominant also intrigued me.

My reading began to take the shape of a conversation with both the dominant voices and the marginal, innovative voices in the literature. At times I read and listened to those theories described or assumed in most of the homiletical literature. I tried to listen carefully and respectively, not wanting to lampoon, belittle, or discard those theories that some of my students and countless preachers in the past and present have found helpful for their preaching. Having listened, I then took time to respond, to ponder why these claims for preaching are problematic for me and for a number of other scholars, pastors, seminarians, and laypersons. This conversation with the dominant understandings of preaching provides the shape and content of chapters 1–3.

At other times when I turned to the literature, I listened to the new or marginal voices that offer alternative understandings more congenial with what I believe. I began to pull these voices together in an effort to clarify my and others' experiences and convictions relating to preaching. This conversation provides the heart of chapter 4.

As I mulled over and responded to what I was reading and as I continued to formulate my alternative insights about preaching, I was "reflecting upon praxis which already exists," a methodology characteristic of feminist theology (Halkes 1980, 114). My conversations with the homiletical literature became the occasion for articulating and analyzing my own and others' experiences of preaching. At the same time I knew that writers outside the field of homiletics were describing practices and hopes that coincide with my descriptions of conversational preaching. In chapter 5 my listening and responding includes voices not at the homiletical table.

Reflection on existing praxis, important in itself for validating our experiences and practices, also potentially serves the larger project of reimaging and enriching homiletics. Theologian Catherina Halkes describes the goal of reflective analysis in theology: "Analysing the praxis . . . leads to critical questions, reformulations, and the liberation and enrichment of theology itself" (114). I have listened to the dominant voices; I have reflected on how I and some others preach; I have asked critical questions and offered an alternative proposal about preaching in the hope that my analysis and reformulations will contribute to the enrichment of homiletics as a multifaceted conversation. As a proposal for one style of preaching, my conversational understanding of preaching seeks to enter the homiletical conversation as an addition to, not a replacement for, existing understandings of preaching.

Essential in my journey to rethink preaching has been the following conviction: nonhierarchical, heuristic, and communal preaching rooted in a relationship of connectedness and mutuality between the preacher and the worshipers already exists as the practice of some preachers. My descriptions of such preaching in chapter 4 propose understandings of preaching's purpose, content, and the technical elements of language and form that are different from the dominant views summarized and evaluated in chapters 1–3. I will summarize here the contours of my conversational understanding of preaching.

Conversational Preaching:
A New Why

In my proposal, preaching's goal is to gather the community of faith around the Word where the central conversations of the church are refocused and fostered. In conversational preaching, the preacher and the congregation are colleagues, exploring together the mystery of the Word for their own lives, as well as the life of the congregation, the larger church, and the world. The preacher and the congregation gather symbolically at a round table without head or foot, where labels like clergy and laity disappear and where believing or wanting to believe is all that matters. Here the preacher is neither the expert in scriptural interpretation nor the answer-person in matters of faith. Here the preacher is simply the one responsible for putting the text and the sermon as one interpretation into the midst of the community for the particular service of worship. Although one person usually does all the speaking during the time set aside for the sermon, exploring the Word and deciding its meanings, its claims, and its direction-pointings are the responsibilities of the priesthood of all believers—that is, the entire community of faith both locally and globally. Conversational preaching aims to gather the local community of faith service after service, week after week, year after year, around the Word.

Conversational preaching also aims to nurture the central conversations of the church. These essential conversations are multiple.

They include the divine-human conversations between the community of faith, a people with a semblance of distinctive identity and communal agenda, and the Word as found in all its complexity and elusiveness in scriptural texts. They include the divine-human conversations between the community of faith and God, the foremost character in our ongoing "small" stories as the covenant people. These divine-human conversations also include the Word of God in partnership with individual believers, each with an unrepeatable configuration of personal stories and webs of storied relationships.

These essential conversations also include human-human conversations. These, too, are multifaceted, expanding from the preaching moment in ever-widening circles. These conversation partners include those who preach and those who do not, those who are confident in matters of faith and those who find themselves awkward and unsure, those for whom church is a second home and those who rarely set foot in institutionalized holy space, those who are "like us" and those whose ideas come from "off the wall" or "out of left field," those who are glib and those who are mute, those who are successful in the eyes of the world and those whose true selves have been slammed and silenced. Conversational preaching seeks to gather together these voices—local and global, present and past—paying particular attention to those that have been drowned out by the din around the round and the rectangular tables of our world, paying particular attention to the whispers and the pauses where people's voices are missing. Conversational preaching wrestles with Word and words, with Silence and silence, seeking to invite everyone to participate in those life-giving conversations that make up the ongoing stories of God's people.

This why of conversational preaching—to gather the community of faith around the Word where the central conversations of the church are refocused and fostered—demands new whats and new hows.

Conversational Preaching:
New Whats and Hows

In the dominant understandings of preaching, the content of sermons is usually truth—variously identified as universal, kerygmatic, or existential. Contemporary insights into the limitations of language and realizations that old formulations of truth or the Word have excluded many people from the formative theological and homiletical conversations have convinced me that no "truth" is objective, absolute, ontological, or archetypal. The only way I can speak of "truth" is eschatologically. The Day will come when we will understand, but until that Day we live by faith and hope, not by sure knowledge, clear facts, or unambiguous truth.

What then is the content of preaching when every articulation of faith and every experience, including experiences of grace and the gospel, are colored and textured by the race, gender, class, nationality, age, personality type, education, and the list goes on, of the one articulating and experiencing? Does preaching's content slide into the quagmire of relativism where everything is slippery and unstable? No. In conversational preaching, a sermon's content is a proposal offered to the community of faith for their additions, corrections, or counterproposals. A sermon's content is a tentative interpretation of Scripture that acknowledges, as best it can, its limitations and biases. Most important, a sermon's content is a wager on the part of the preacher: a new insight that has brought comfort or challenge; an old faith claim revisited in new life circumstances; a resting-place, oasis, or scenic overlook along the congregation's or the preacher's pilgrimage with the Spirit. In conversational preaching, the preacher searches for meaning arising at the intersection of a text and life's myriad experiences. The preacher searches for meaning that makes life livable and, by the secret workings of the Spirit, grace-filled. This meaning is then submitted to the community of faith through the sermon for their answering meanings. One meaning funds multiple meanings, one experience of grace funds multiple experiences of grace, one proposed articulation of the gospel funds multiple articulations of the gospel, through the Spirit that prods and prompts the hearts and minds of the congregation.

This centrifugal movement of preaching is answered, and probably preceded, by a centripetal movement. Sermon after sermon, service after service, the Spirit is shaping for God a people who in fits and fractures give evidence of a common hope that God's promised shalom is worth our living and our dying; who, however discordantly or contrapuntally, raise a collective voice that glorifies God. Through time, the Spirit weaves together the threads of multiple meanings, variegated experiences of grace, and diverse articulations of the gospel to fashion and refashion worshipers into a people who belong to God.

Conversational preaching flows from faith and hope into faith and hope, struggling to discern the ever-changing patterns in the indistinct mirrors called Word, truth, gospel, or revelation, through which we now see dimly and distortedly. Conversational preaching is faithful not in relation to some "objective" or "absolute" standard of Word, truth, gospel, or revelation, but in relation to the health of the multiple conversations that *all* contribute to the formation and reformation of God's people on our way toward the eschaton where we believe and hope we will see God face-to-face.

Reformulations of preaching's why and what work hand in hand with new hows. I will say a brief word about sermonic language and then sermonic forms.

Conversational preaching offers an alternative to two standard "rules" about sermonic language. The traditional rule is that sermonic language should be clear to ensure that the preacher's message is accurately transmitted. A more contemporary rule is that sermonic language should be poetic, evocative, and performative—that is, capable of performing the activity to which it refers—to ensure that the preacher's experience of the text or an experience purported to be encoded in the text is reenacted in the congregation. These understandings presuppose a hierarchy that privileges the preacher's knowledge or experience above the congregation's knowledge or experience.

Conversational preaching, however, values poetic, evocative language for a different reason. Such language is able to invite to the sermonic round table the experiences, thoughts, and wagers of all those present and even of those absent.

In addition, conversational preaching values the confessional language of the community of believers as it is rethought and reclaimed time and again. Sermonic words that are poetic and confessional remind the worshipers of their own lives, limitations, sins, moments of grace, and named or unnamed glimpses of the Spirit at work. Sermonic metaphors and images play along the edge of what we know of God's Mystery. Sermonic words that arise from the age-old experiences of God's seeking-to-be-faithful people are set beside the depths of contemporary human experiences where they dance from our deeps to the surface and back, from our centers to the periphery and back, inviting Mystery to be a part of our always-too-small stories.

The how of conversational preaching also involves sermonic form. Inductive sermons, as described by Fred B. Craddock, and narrative sermons, as described by Eugene L. Lowry, are potentially heuristic forms that invite the congregation to work out their own meanings in a give-and-take with the Spirit. The worshipers need not take the particular journey presented by the preacher.

Rather, through inductive and narrative forms sermons offer possibilities that intentionally fund a wealth of possibilities.

In addition, the story-sermon is potentially a heuristic form that allows the worshipers to overhear multivalent proposals, interpretations, or wagers and, by the aid of the Spirit, decide their own conclusions. Other sermonic forms that suggest, propose, and evoke also potentially fund conversational preaching.

This, in summary, is my proposal for a conversational understanding of preaching. It builds on insights already present in recent homiletical literature and on the practice of many of us who preach and worship within communities of faith. The term *proposal* is important to me, for it implies the constant need for the enlargement, the confirmation, as well as the correction of other descriptions of preaching in the larger conversation called homiletics.

Homiletics as a Conversation:
Probe One

Several times in this Introduction I have referred to homiletics—that is, thinking and writing about the practices of preaching—as a conversation among divergent theories and proposals. My conviction is that no single theory or set of understandings defines preaching and its tasks. This image of homiletics as a conversation deserves a closer look.

What do I mean by the expression "homiletics as a conversation"? The expression implies a particular story of homiletical theory in the twentieth century. This story charts a shift from one consensus to a second consensus to no consensus. Very briefly, the story goes like this. During the first half of this century, John A. Broadus's *On the Preparation and Delivery of Sermons* dominated the teaching of homiletics. Just prior to the turn of the century, in 1897, this book was hailed as "the most popular and wide-read text-book on Homiletics in this country" (Broadus and Weatherspoon 1944, vii). Revising this classic in 1944, Jesse Burton Weatherspoon claimed that "the book has been in constant and increasing use since its first appearance and . . . remains the outstanding text-book of Homiletics" (v). Not until 1958 was its dominance seriously challenged. Roughly, the first half of this century could be designated the Broadus era, and this understanding of preaching continues to influence homiletical theory today as the dominant backdrop against which contemporary traditional homiletical theory is formulated.

In 1958, a second era began with the publication of H. Grady Davis's *Design for Preaching*. Before long this book had ousted Broadus's as the leading textbook. In a survey of preaching professors in 1974, over half of the respondents selected Davis's *Design for Preaching* as their textbook of choice (Chatfield 1984, 2). Between 1958 and 1974, the earlier consensus that had looked to Broadus to define the tasks of preaching had dissolved and a new consensus had formed around Davis.

Davis is primarily a theorist and encyclopedist of sermonic forms. His *Design for Preaching* anticipates and charts the course for many of the discussions of sermon forms that have characterized homiletical thinking in recent years. My own discussions of him appear in chapters 3 and 4, where I discuss his transformational understandings of preaching and his innovative thinking about sermonic forms.

If *Design for Preaching* was the most popular textbook in 1974, by 1984 its dominance had waned, and concurrently so had the dominance of any single textbook. According to a second survey in 1984, only five of the forty-six respondents, or 12 percent, listed Davis's *Design for Preaching* as a textbook they used in their preaching courses (ibid.). Although the Davis consensus had dissipated, no other book had arisen to take its place. Respondents were asked in the survey, "What basic textbooks do you use, if any?" A total of 115 books were listed, and no book was mentioned more than seven times (ibid., 1). Into this disarray, between 1985 and 1989 came ten textbooks that attempted to consolidate the best of the field.[2] Yet no new consensus has emerged.

This story of homiletics claims that for roughly three-quarters of the twentieth-century scholars and preachers generally agreed about correct homiletical theory. Broadus represents the earlier state of the art and Davis the later. Then between 1974 and 1984 consensus disappeared.[3] The 1980s became an era in which homiletical scholarship tried at times to reclaim an earlier consensus and at other times to articulate a new position around which to rally a new consensus. Consensus, however, remained an elusive goal.

This story of homiletical theory thus ends with the dissipation of agreed-upon norms and, for some, a search for consensus. Along my journey, as I began to identify the contours of an alternative understanding of preaching, I found myself leery of a new consensus, even one defined by my own convictions. Early on I knew that the conversational understanding of preaching coalescing in my mind from bits and pieces I was gleaning from the homiletical literature is not the only understanding of preaching. It is one among a number of attempts to describe what preaching is all about. It is a particular model that seeks to represent a valid but different way some of us experience ourselves in the pulpit and the pew, in the church, and in the world. The image of homiletics as a conversation invites a give-and-take among a variety of interpretations of preaching.

Homiletics as a Conversation:
Probe Two

Again, what do I mean by the expression "homiletics as a conversation"? The expression also implies a particular range of meanings for the word *conversation*. Don Browning borrows the following four elements of a good conversation from Hans-Georg Gadamer:

First, people who converse are located in particular social and historical locations. They have particular concerns and unique experiences and questions. They bring these situated experiences and questions into the conversation. Second, people in conversations generally share something in common; it may be their common humanity, but it is also likely to be some shared historical experience to which they both can make reference. Third, conversations have a give-and-take quality to them; they are in this respect almost like play. Fourth, people in conversations also have to listen to the other in openness and be willing to take the risk that the other may have something important—possibly even transforming—to say. Being open to this transformation does not mean we suppress our own experiences, questions, and concerns. In fact, it is likely that the truth the other speaks will be understood as meaningful, real, relevant, and indeed revelatory only in light of our concerns and questions. (1994, 131)

Browning's description of a conversation is similar to "really talking" in *Women's Ways of Knowing:*

"Really talking" . . . implies mutually shared agreement that together you are creating the optimum setting so that half-baked or emergent ideas can grow. "Real talk" reaches deep into the experience of each participant; it also draws on the analytical abilities of each. Conversation . . . includes discourse and exploration, talking and listening, questions, argument, speculation, and sharing. (Belenky and others 1986, 144)

Women's Ways of Knowing also describes conversations as "intimate rather than impersonal, relatively informal and unstructured rather than bound by more or less explicit formal rules" (114).

I lift up these two descriptions of the word *conversation* in order to distinguish my range of meanings from David Tracy's more technical definition (1987). Tracy follows Gadamer more narrowly than Browning and defines conversation as discourse focused on a common subject matter or a particular question under consideration (19, 20). For Tracy, conversation is a "game" played by "some hard rules" (19). In this game, friendship yields, the subject matter takes over, and the participants lose themselves in the pursuit of truth (19). The final goal of the game, according to Tracy, is new consensus (98).

My understanding of conversation is more informal and personal than Tracy's.[4] Key characteristics for me include an atmosphere of openness and mutual respect, as well as the willingness of the participants to acknowledge the particularity of their experiences based on their historical and social locations. My hope is that the image of homiletics as a conversation will further efforts in the field of homiletics to identify and respect a broad range of differences and to make room for a variety of homiletical theories reflecting a variety of experiences, theologies, and ecclesiologies.

I offer this book as an "emergent" (Belenky and others 1986, 144) proposal that now enters into conversation with the larger community of the church and the academy. Tracy suggests that "when there are no further relevant questions either from the text or from myself or from the interaction that is questioning, . . . I then present my interpretation to the community of inquiry to see if they have further relevant questions" (1987, 25).

Using Tracy's language, I have engaged in an extended process of "interaction that is questioning" (ibid.). I have interacted, on the one hand, with the literature of homiletical theory—the dominant and the marginal voices—and, on the other hand, with the experiences of some of us who sit in the pew or preach, yet who do not find those experiences taken seriously by current understandings of preaching. Unlike Tracy, however, I cannot claim to have laid all the questions to rest. The generative questions that initiated my journey have found no definitive answers. Rather, they have found temporary settlement in this proposal. At the same time I am ready to "present my interpretation" (ibid.) to others who have also been reflecting on what preaching is all about. Again in Tracy's words, "To make a claim is to be willing to defend that claim if challenged by others or by the further process of questioning itself" (ibid.). I am now willing to defend my claims and, I hope, to rethink them in conversations with others.

To My Readers

To those readers who espouse one of the dominant views of preaching, I ask that you listen to my proposal. I resonate with Halkes, who invites other theologians into the "dialogue" of theology (1980, 120) in which the goal is not "victory" for one and "defeat" for the other but "mutual enrichment through mutual understanding" (121). I invite my colleagues in the church and the academy to listen and respond for our "mutual enrichment" (ibid.).

And perhaps some readers are searching for and formulating alternative understandings of preaching. I welcome these responses as well. My prayer is that some readers will recognize themselves in what I say because I am struggling to put into words what we together already fervently, although still sometimes inchoately, believe.[5]

The House That Fear Built:
Warsaw, 1943

Jane Flanders

The purpose of poetry is to remind us how difficult it is to remain just one person, for our house is open, there are no keys in the doors.

—*Czeslaw Milosz*

*I am the boy with his hands raised over his head
in Warsaw.*

*I am the soldier whose rifle is trained
on the boy with his hands raised over his head
in Warsaw.*

*I am the woman with lowered gaze
who fears the soldier whose rifle is trained
on the boy with his hands raised over his head
in Warsaw.*

*I am the man in the overcoat
who loves the woman with lowered gaze
who fears the soldier whose rifle is trained
on the boy with his hands raised over his head
in Warsaw.*

I am the stranger who photographs
the man in the overcoat
who loves the woman with lowered gaze
who fears the soldier whose rifle is trained
on the boy with his hands raised over his head
in Warsaw.

The crowd, of which I am each part, moves on
beneath my window, for I am the crone too
who shakes her sheets
over every street in the world
muttering
What's this? What's this?

from *Meditations with Julian of Norwich*

Julian of Norwich

God wants to be thought of
as our Lover.
I must see myself so bound in love
as if everything that has been done
has been done for me.
That is to say,
the Love of God makes such a unity in us
that when we see this unity
no one is able to separate oneself
from another.

1 ∞ Homiletics' Elder Statesman Speaks

You're sitting in a pew on a Sunday morning. The preacher is entering the pulpit: What do you expect from the sermon? Later you realize the sermon was meaningful: Was there something memorable or provocative about its content, language, or form?

Or you're standing in a pulpit about to preach: What do you believe you are doing? Later someone asks you about your understanding of preaching: How do you describe its purpose, content, language, or form? What *is* this ecclesial practice called preaching?

Today no single description of preaching provides standard answers to these questions. No consensus, as in the past, offers ready answers.

Instead, thinking about preaching today resembles a conversation among divergent points of view. My hope is that the aim of our conversation will not be a new consensus or the declaration of a winner but increased understanding of the differences and commonalities among our viewpoints and an enrichment of both preaching and reflection about preaching.

In today's homiletical conversation there are three dominant voices. Before I interject an additional perspective, I suggest we listen respectfully to those voices that have for years sought to describe preaching. In other words, I want to acknowledge that the homiletical conversation is already in progress. While listening, however, I also want to evaluate the claims of the dominant voices against my own and others' experiences and convictions. It is clear to many of us that the homiletical conversation already in progress has not taken seriously our experiences and beliefs about preaching.

One of the longest-standing, dominant voices at the homiletical table is traditional or classic theory that is grounded in homiletical rhetoric. This theory, which is the topic of this chapter, continues the legacy of John A. Broadus, whose 1870 textbook defined preaching for the first half of the twentieth century. Or perhaps more accurately, this tradition extends further back into history to Augustine (354–430 C.E.) and his homiletical theory that joined Christian preaching and classical rhetoric. Throughout the nearly two thousand years of Christian preaching, traditional theory has shifted its boundaries and its emphases; yet much has remained the same.

Traditional homiletical theory is not likely to go out of style anytime soon in textbooks for seminary students or in books for seasoned preachers. Although its claims have sometimes been presented as clear-cut and final, in actuality it has changed over the years as a result of its encounters with an ever-changing world and an ever-changing church. Traditional homiletical theory will most likely continue to shape and be reshaped by preachers who deliver sermons week after week and year after year.

In addition, some students arrive at seminary with skills for preaching traditional sermons. Their emerging styles remain commensurate with their life experiences and their convictions about themselves, the church, and the Word of God. As developing preachers, they need, in part, to hone their skills according to the best of traditional homiletical theory.

For these students and preachers, traditional theory is a fit; for others of us, it is not. We have felt crimped by its implicit one-size-fits-all. Traditional theory has been a glass slipper that does not slip perfectly onto our feet. We have been stepsisters, tempted to cut off a big toe or a wide heel to force our foot into Cinderella's slipper.[1] Or to change the story, Procrustes' bed does not fit every traveler. In this story from Greek mythology, Procrustes insisted that all his boarders fit into his bed. When they were too tall, he chopped off their legs; when they were too short, he stretched them to fit. In either case, the self-mutilation or violence may in no way have been the intention of homiletical scholars or professors, but the normative power of traditional homiletical theory has been hard for some of us to resist.

What is this powerful voice in the homiletical conversation? And why is it sometimes not a fit? In seeking answers to these questions I find myself hoping that homiletics, like a department store, will offer a variety of sizes and shapes of slippers and beds.

Listening to
Traditional Theory

Traditional homiletical theory has a particular set of norms regarding preaching's purpose, content, and such technical elements as language and form. Behind each set of norms hovers Broadus's theory, as it was revised by Jesse Burton Weatherspoon in 1944. At the same time, each set of norms has been reformulated as traditional theory has shifted and broadened in recent years.

Purpose

According to Broadus and Weatherspoon, preaching's purpose, like that of rhetoric or oratory, is persuasion. Traditional homiletical theory envisions the preacher as the authority figure whose "main duty is to tell people what to believe and why they should believe it" (1944, 157). Preachers should also aim "to teach God's Word" (16); their "very purpose" is "teaching and exhorting [the people] out of the Word of God" (24). At the same time, Broadus and Weatherspoon oppose the image of the preacher as "a dignitary, speaking ex cathedra to inferiors" (213). Rather than remaining "at a distance," the preacher should be "a witness and fellow-worshiper" (10). Such a stance aids the preacher's ability to persuade because understanding the congregation and sympathizing with them increases the preacher's persuasive power.

In the literature of contemporary traditional theory, the word *persuade* continues to be a popular description of preaching's purpose. Almost as popular is the word *transmit*: the preacher's goal is to transmit the sermon's truth or message to the congregation.[2] Other words associated with this understanding are *convince, inform, explain,* and *communicate*. The preacher has some insight or belief that the congregation needs to understand and accept. In some contemporary versions of traditional theory, the preacher receives the message or truth and passes it along to the congregation. The preacher thus is the conduit between the Word of God, the Bible, the ecclesiastical tradition, or the Spirit, on the one hand, and the congregation, on the other.

In a nutshell, successful preaching is successful, unadulterated communication. Roy M. Pearson identifies the preacher's task in this way: The preacher wants the congregation "to understand what he is saying as he understands it himself and to interpret his words, as he himself interprets them" (1962, 162). James W. Cox echoes this understanding:

> The purpose of preaching is to get what is in the mind and heart of the preacher into the mind and heart of the hearer. This suggests that preaching is a one-way street, a one-dimensional kind of communication.
>
> Preaching *is* one-way communication. We have received a message, and we have to pass it on. (1985, 51)

Such an understanding of preaching's purpose presupposes a gap between the pulpit and the pew. This gap is fundamental to the roles assigned to the preacher and the congregation. The preacher is the sender, the communicator, the one with a message or truth to transmit by means of the sermon to the congregation. The congregation consists of recipients. Although they are often described as actively participating in the process, their chief task is to give assent to the sermon's message.[3] Across the gap between the sender and the receivers goes the sermon.

One image of this communicative process is the preacher as the pitcher in a baseball game and the congregation as the catcher (Cleland 1965, 104; Freeman 1987, 11). The language of some scholars is more violent. Pearson borrows an image from the celebrated preacher Henry Ward Beecher. The sermon is like a hunter's gun: "at every discharge [the preacher] should look to see his game fall" (1954, 24). Ralph L. Lewis and Gregg A. Lewis develop Beecher's image of the preacher as "taking aim" at the congregation (1983, 135). They encourage preachers to spend time focusing the sermon because such time "sometimes makes the difference between a shotgun loaded with birdshot and a big-game rifle" (135).

In traditional theory, "getting the message across" (Cox 1985, ix) is preaching's goal, and the preacher's task is to send the message clearly and effectively so that it is "understood, believed, felt, or acted upon" (202).

Content

Traditional homiletical theory also has its own normative understanding of preaching's content. Broadus and Weatherspoon identify the content of preaching as "divine truth" (1944, 6) or "some significant truth bearing upon religious life" (50). This truth that constitutes the sermon's subject should be congruent with "the general teachings of Scripture" (47). Absent or making only rare appearances are such theological terms as *kerygma,* the *Word of God,* and *revelation.* This minor role of terms that are dominant in other understandings of preaching is not surprising, because the larger context for Broadus and Weatherspoon's discussions of preaching is rhetoric, not theology.

A prominent contemporary reformulator of traditional homiletics is James W. Cox. Section III of his textbook *Preaching* (1985) is titled "The Content of Sermons." Here, as in Broadus and Weatherspoon, the word *truth* appears again and again to designate preaching's content. In discerning a sermon's particular content, preachers have two tasks. First, they must study biblical texts for the truth that is relevant for the contemporary situation. This task includes applying "general or universal" truth to particular life situations (70). The second task is formulating the truth of the text into the sermon's central idea so that it can be clearly transmitted, communicated, or imparted to the congregation. Cox claims that, in order for such transmission or communication to happen, the preacher and the congregation must "recognize or posit the existence of objective truth" (54). These assumptions—that truth exists independent of the preacher and that it can be formulated into the sermon's central idea—lead me to designate the content of this theory of preaching as objective, propositional truth.[4]

Undergirding Cox's definition of preaching's content are particular understandings of the *kerygma,* the Word of God, and revelation. These concepts, however, are not fully developed and play minor roles in Cox's theory of preaching. The *kerygma* is the gospel, "the substance of the Christian message" (12), and "the essential message [that] does not change" (11). At times the *kerygma* and truth seem identical. Like truth, the *kerygma* is objective and propositional to the extent that it is a message that the preacher receives and must "pass on unchanged" (8).

Two other key theological and homiletical concepts in terms of preaching's content are God's Word and revelation. For Cox, the Word, like the *kerygma* and truth, exists as an objective reality. It is the power of God at work in creation, history, nature, the message of the Hebrew prophets, the written word of Scripture, and preaching. In addition, God's "decisive and supremely revelatory word" is spoken in Jesus Christ (7). Revelation is the means of communication between the Word of God and the human race. Cox most explicitly discusses the concept of revelation in relation to the Bible. In varying degrees, biblical texts reveal "the heart and mind of God" (66). What the Bible reveals about God is certain and clear so that Cox can evaluate the concept of love in the preaching of Dwight L. Moody and conclude "that [Moody's] concept of love was informed by the way the love of God has been expressed by God himself" (66).

Truth, as the content of preaching in traditional homiletical theory, is objective, waiting to be discovered in God's Word, the Bible, as *kerygma* or revelation. This truth once discovered is propositional; that is, the preacher can state it as the sermon's central idea and, in the effective sermon, transmit it to the congregation for their acceptance.

Language

Traditional homiletics' understandings of the purpose and content of preaching are inextricably linked with presuppositions about language. Once again the ongoing influence of Broadus and Weatherspoon is unmistakable.

Broadus and Weatherspoon insist that "clearness or perspicuity" is of utmost importance in preaching (1944, 240). The goal of such clarity is to aid transmission. As preachers, "we must strive to render it not merely possible that the people should understand us but impossible that they should misunderstand" (96). The words and phrases preachers use, therefore, should "exactly express [their] thought" (244). The general rule is that "terms ought to be precise, . . . so that the expression and the idea exactly correspond, neither of them containing anything which the other does not contain" (244).

Along with clarity, Broadus and Weatherspoon emphasize another important quality of style, force, defined as energy, animation, or passion, which results in a magnetic effect on the congregation. A figure of speech, like a metaphor or synecdoche, may be introduced if it moves the will. The rule regarding sermonic language is "that which does not contribute to perspicuity or force must never be introduced merely as an ornament, for this, as we have seen, belongs to poetry but not to practical and serious discourse" (275).

Like Broadus and Weatherspoon, Cox, a major preserver and reshaper of traditional theory, is primarily concerned that sermonic language be clear. Concern for clarity is related to his definition of preaching's purpose: "Clarity of expression determines clarity of understanding" (1985, 219). Therefore, Cox offers rules by which preachers can choose those "words that will most quickly and surely convey our meaning" (219). Figures of speech, such as similes and metaphors, are useful only as long as they contribute to the development of the sermon's central idea. The underlying conviction is that if language is clear, what the preacher sends will be identical to what the congregation receives. What the preacher sends and what the congregation receives should cohere in precise words that accurately present the truth to which they refer. Words that are precise can grasp and deliver objective truth.

Other homiletical scholars who espouse traditional theory share, sometimes explicitly and sometimes implicitly, similar assumptions about language and particularly sermonic language. The underlying attitude is one of confidence: confidence that preachers can choose words so that "the expression and the idea exactly correspond" (Broadus and Weatherspoon 1944, 244); confidence that words can convey truth; and confidence that the communication process is trustworthy if language is clear.

Form

No single form characterizes traditional homiletics. An unfair caricature equates traditional homiletical theory with "three points and a poem." Two issues in recent discussions of form by traditional theorists are noteworthy. The first is the importance they place on formulating the content or truth of the sermon into a single sentence or idea.[5] The second is an appropriation of narrative and inductive sermon forms. Whereas Broadus and Weatherspoon and most other traditional scholars relegate narration and induction to supportive roles in preaching, several traditional scholars discuss their use as processes for shaping the entire sermon.

Traditional homiletics insists that a sermon's effectiveness is enhanced when the preacher can clearly summarize the sermon's message or truth into a single sentence. For the preacher, this focus sentence is helpful because it gives coherence and direction to the shape the sermon takes. For the congregation, the focus sentence is helpful because it enables them more readily to grasp the preacher's meaning.

Broadus and Weatherspoon's label for this summary of the sermon's message is "the proposition" (1944, 54). It "is a statement of the subject as the preacher proposes to develop it. It is subject (idea) and predicate. The subject answers the question, What is the sermon about?" (54). Together the subject and the predicate form "one complete declarative sentence, simple, clear, and cogent" (55), which states "the gist of the sermon" (56).

Cox's corresponding term is the "central idea," which consists of both a subject and a predicate (1985, 79). In language that echoes Broadus and Weatherspoon, Cox claims that the subject is an answer to the question, "What is the preacher talking about?" (79). The subject and the predicate together constitute "the gist of the sermon, the sermon in a nutshell" (79).

The importance of the focus statement, proposition, or central idea is a legacy of traditional homiletics that has an almost ironclad hold on preaching. One scholar claims:

> One of the most hallowed homiletical axioms is that the preacher should be able to put into one sentence the essence of the sermon. That sentence is

called the sermon's thesis, proposition, generative idea, big truth, subject sentence, sermon-in-a-nutshell, or main point. . . . The central, controlling idea is not an option but an urgent necessity. (Thompson 1981, 91)

A second issue that is noteworthy in discussions of form in traditional homiletical theory is the role of narration and induction. The most typical position is that of Broadus and Weatherspoon, where both narration and induction are assigned subordinate roles in the sermon-making process. Broadus and Weatherspoon describe four means for developing the sermon: argument, explanation, application, and illustration (1944, 155). Induction is a subcategory under argument. Narration is a subcategory chiefly under explanation, although it may also help a preacher apply or illustrate a truth or idea.

For Broadus and Weatherspoon, induction, as a type of argument, at its best offers the "particulars" that provide the basis for a conclusion. It constructs "strong bridges of facts" that lead "to some significant realization" (177). At its worst, it draws a general conclusion from a few examples or superficial observation and results in "ten thousand erroneous inductions" (177). The preacher must be careful to engage in "safe induction" that consists not only in "aggregat[ing] a number of instances" but also in analyzing and comparing them (176).

For Broadus and Weatherspoon, narration also plays a supportive role: narration must "always [be] subordinate . . . to . . . the conviction or persuasion which [the preacher] wishes to effect" (159).

Regarding biblical stories, the usual expectation is that preachers should "not elaborate or enlarge upon some [biblical] narrative merely because it is in itself interesting, or follow the story step by step according to its own laws" (159). A somewhat different understanding of the use of biblical narrative material emerges from Broadus and Weatherspoon's discussion of expository preaching. One class of expository preaching "spends much time in bringing out clearly and vividly the [biblical] scene or story" (144). At the same time, such preaching should balance the telling of the story and "the lessons which the narrative teaches" (145). Two dangers exist. The expository preacher should not focus on the lessons derived from the passage and ignore "the narrative, with all its charm" (145); nor should the expository preacher practice "word-painting," that is, adding "elaborate descriptions" to "the simple and beautiful Scripture story," and ignore the story's lessons (145). Broadus and Weatherspoon's concern is "that there ought to be such a method of preaching upon the narrative portions of Scripture as should be distinctively appropriate to narrative, while yet it is preaching" (145).

Harold Freeman is a traditional scholar who shifts narrative from its supportive role to a different status as a sermonic form (1987). As though in answer to Broadus and Weatherspoon's concern for "a method of preaching upon the narrative portions of Scripture" that is "distinctively appropriate to narrative, while yet it is preaching" (1944, 145), Freeman offers the biblical story-sermon.

For Freeman, the first essential task in composing a story-sermon is no different from that of any other sermon—discerning in the biblical passage the sermon's message. When the biblical passage is a narrative, the preacher should begin with the intention of the biblical storyteller and then structure the sermon along the lines of the biblical story. Freeman also gives other options, including discerning the message in several narrative passages, non-narrative passages, or an imagined situation. What is imperative is that the preacher "identify the point of the story," because "there's no point in telling the story unless the people get the point, and they won't get the point unless *you* get the point" (137). In these descriptions of the narrative message, the principles of traditional theory are normative. The purpose of preaching is for the congregation to give assent to the sermon's message. And the content of preaching, the sermon's message, is the eternal truth or truths embedded in the biblical narrative by its author (140).

Freeman's second task is constructing the sermon as a story that transmits that message to the congregation. He gives the following advice:

> If the message is to be accurately perceived, you may need to articulate clearly the principle(s) or truth(s) conveyed by the story. This can be done without getting into detailed, lengthy application of the truth to the various areas of the lives of the hearers. Just focus on the main truth. (152)

It is clear that for Freeman the story, or narrative sermon, is a strategy whereby the preacher communicates a biblical truth to the congregation.

Like Freeman, a traditional scholar who elevates narrative to the status of a sermonic form, Ralph Loren Lewis and Gregg A. Lewis are traditional scholars who elevate the inductive process to the status of a sermonic form (1983). For Lewis and Lewis, the inductive process is the reverse of the deductive process. Inductive preaching, therefore, is the reverse of deductive preaching. The deductive sermon begins with a statement of truth and then seeks to convince the congregation of its validity, using illustrations and facts as proof. The movement is from the general to the particulars. The inductive sermon begins with the particulars—"the narrative, dialogue, analogy, questions, parables, the concrete experiences"—and invites the congregation to think along with the preacher, "to weigh the evidence, think through the implications and then come to the conclusion *with* the preacher at the end of the sermon" (43). The movement is from the particulars to the general. According to Lewis and Lewis, by the end of the inductive sermon the congregation will recognize that the sermon's concluding truth agrees with their understanding of the facts and their own life experiences. They will be ready to accept the sermon's conclusion.

What situates this description of inductive preaching wholly within traditional homiletical theory is this understanding of the conclusion. Although the congregation is invited to participate in the sermon, to think with and even ahead of the preacher's thoughts, at the end of the successful sermon the preacher and the congregation arrive at the same conclusion. Lewis and Lewis reiterate the importance of "making certain the people get where we want them to be, that they reach our corporate concept, that they believe and accept that conclusion and are ready then for us to go on to declare, elaborate on, reaffirm and apply that message deductively" (136). Inductive structure for Lewis and Lewis is a strategy that leads the congregation to the conclusion "the preacher wants to get across" (100), a conclusion that should be grounded in God's eternal truth (108, 112).

In these descriptions of narrative sermons by Freeman and inductive sermons by Lewis and Lewis, traditional homiletics remains normative. Preachers who choose narrative and inductive sermon forms must follow the rule of stating the sermon's message succinctly, because such a statement increases the likelihood that the congregation will receive the sermon's truth. Narrative and inductive sermon forms thus serve traditional preaching's purpose and content; they are strategies for winning the congregation's assent to the sermon's message.

Responding

Traditional homiletical theory underscores the fact that sermons do function to inculcate and transmit Christian beliefs. When the persuasive communication of a faith claim is the primary task that the preacher sets for the sermon, then traditional homiletical theory may aid the preacher in that task. For example, a sermon's explicit purpose might be to elicit assent to a particular doctrinal formulation, to challenge heresy, or to persuade the congregation to act justly or kindly. Then traditional theory may provide the preacher with helpful tools. Traditional sermons are also effective in leading worshipers to celebrate, reclaim, or grasp more deeply beliefs and practices already held by the community of faith.

In addition, traditional homiletical theory supports the expectations and suits the personalities of some pastors, seminarians, and congregations. It is a particularly good fit for those who see the preacher as the authority figure and the authoritative interpreter of Scripture and life for the community of faith.

Yet for others of us—laypersons, pastors, seminarians, and homiletical scholars—traditional theory is problematic. The four responses that follow highlight four problems that prohibit traditional theory's being a fit for some of us.

Response One: The Gap Between Preacher and Congregation

The most fundamental problem with traditional theory is that it is predicated on a gap that separates the preacher and the congregation. This gap does not reflect the primary relationship that some of us experience as preachers and members of congregations.[6] Rather, for us the primary relationship is solidarity and mutuality. Our image of preaching does not presuppose a sense of separation between the preacher as sender and the congregation as recipients. Instead, more fundamental than differences between the preacher and the congregation are experiences of belonging, shared identity, and mutual interdependency. Because traditional homiletical theory presupposes a gap that separates the preacher and the worshipers, it is incapable of taking seriously alternative experiences that are rooted in connectedness.

Hand in hand with this gap in traditional theory are the problematic roles assigned to the preacher and the congregation. Some of us are wary of the preacher's role as the community's primary authority figure, answer-person, or authoritative interpreter of Scripture and life. We are also wary of the congregation's role as recipients, however active they may be in the sermon process, because of the possibility that certain members of the community may remain passive and dependent on the preacher to tell them what to be, think, or do. For us, a sermon is not by definition the vehicle for a message or truth that the preacher receives and transmits to the congregation for acceptance or rejection.

Challenging traditional theory, Christine M. Smith (1989) claims that the preacher and the worshiping community are not "separate and distinct realities" (57). Preaching, she asserts, is not grounded in the preacher's "special rights, power, knowledge, and capacity to influence or transform" (46). Instead, Smith's concern is an understanding of preaching that is grounded in mutuality and solidarity between the preacher and the community.

Like Smith, I am aware that for many of us—pastors, laypersons, and seminarians—the preacher and the congregation are not separate or distinct. As preachers, we have not discovered techniques that bridge the gap—for example, pre-sermon discussions or inductive form. Rather, connectedness is our primary way of being in the world and particularly in the church; thus our approach to preaching is rooted in connectedness.

A number of recent scholars distinguish between connectedness and separation as two fundamental and distinct orientations to life. I will summarize three works by feminist scholars who describe connected and separate ways of being in the world. Because these scholars ascribe the connected mode to women and the separate mode to men, I will use their language in summarizing their convictions. However, after each summary, I will reinterpret their conclusions as pertaining to both women and men, a reinterpretation that accords both with their own claims and with my own experiences.[7] My conviction is that when a connected orientation to life, or to being among believers, constitutes the primary relationship between the preacher and the congregation, this sense of connectedness radically alters the perception of what preaching is about and necessitates new descriptions of preaching.

Carol Gilligan, in her feminist classic *In a Different Voice: Psychological Theory and Women's Development* (1982), challenges the reigning psychological and moral theories describing "human" development. She argues that these theories, because they are based on studies of boys and men, describe male development only. Studies of girls' and women's behavior reveal, she argues, an alternative developmental journey for females.[8] Her conclusion is that the dominant theme of male development is separation, whereas the dominant theme of female development is attachment.

One major theorist whom Gilligan challenges is Erik Erikson. Erikson bases this theory of psychological development on eight stages that the individual must successively negotiate between birth and old age. The pattern of the stages, he claims, is unalterable. According to Gilligan, Erikson's description of both the stages and their sequence presupposes that healthy individuals must separate themselves from others in order to acquire an autonomous sense of identity. According to Gilligan, the theme of separation begins with Erikson's description of stage two when normal children begin to walk and to explore their world. In Erikson's theory, this stage "marks the walking child's emerging sense of separateness and agency" (12). The next two stages contribute to the child's developing sense of separation until the child reaches stage five, adolescence, with its "celebration of the autonomous, initiating, industrious self through the forging of an identity" (12). Gilligan summarizes Erikson's theory as progression toward "autonomy and independence" so that "separation itself becomes the model and the measure of growth" (98).

Gilligan does not argue with Erikson's theory as an accurate description of male development. The centerpiece of Erikson's theory is stage five, which focuses on the adolescent's struggle to form an adequate, autonomous sense of identity. Other scholars have researched Erikson's later stages by studying adult males. Summarizing these studies, Gilligan highlights the liabilities of the Eriksonian developmental journey grounded in separation. These studies reflect the experiences of men who successfully negotiated the early Eriksonian stages and arrived at a sense of separate identity. But Gilligan contends that, according to the data, these men are poorly equipped to negotiate the adult crisis of intimacy versus isolation, stage six. They evidence a failure to develop healthy relationships and to advance toward "a maturity of interdependence" (155). In their aiming toward "individuation and achievement," they have subordinated their ability to form relationships and "constricted their emotional expression" (154). While successfully achieving a separate identity, they have lost the ability to form intimate relationships.

Gilligan's argument is that "human" developmental theories are based on male experiences as the normative data. Such theories chart development as progression toward autonomy and individuation that culminates in a sense of self that is distinct from the world and other people (46–47).

Gilligan's significant contribution to developmental theory and feminist literature is to propose an alternative theory of development based on attachment.[9] Relying on studies by Nancy Chodorow, Gilligan begins her counter theory with the infant girl whose primary caregiver is a woman. The girl develops not by separating herself from the female caregiver, as a boy does, but by recognizing a fundamental connectedness that shapes her emerging sense of self. Summarizing and quoting Chodorow, Gilligan writes of both modes of development:

> Female identity formation takes place in a context of ongoing relationship since "mothers tend to experience their daughters as more like, and continuous with, themselves." Correspondingly, girls, in identifying themselves as female, experience themselves as like their mothers, thus fusing this experience of attachment with the process of identity formation. In contrast, "mothers experience their sons as a male opposite," and boys, in defining themselves as masculine, separate their mothers from themselves, thus curtailing, "their primary love and sense of empathic tie." Consequently, male development entails a "more emphatic individuation and a more defensive firming of experienced ego boundaries."[10]

Gilligan continues to trace the development of girls in contrast to that of boys by citing other studies. These studies demonstrate that girls' games differ from boys' games (9–10) and that girls' values, by which they make ethical decisions, differ from those of boys (25–39). In these studies, Gilligan claims the differences between girls and boys reflect different self-understandings. Girls identify themselves through their relationships to others and value an ethic of care based on the continuity of those relationships. Boys, on the other hand, identify themselves through their sense of separation from others and as a result both welcome disputes as a part of the game and value rules and abstract ideals to help them resolve their disputes and moral dilemmas.

When girls arrive at puberty and move into adulthood, Gilligan argues, they are at a disadvantage because the norm against which they are judged is based on male development. This "adult" norm consists of "the capacity for autonomous thinking, clear decision-making, and responsible action" (17). This norm "favor[s] the separateness of the individual self over connection to others, and lean[s] more toward an autonomous life of work than toward the interdependence of love and care" (17). Gilligan suggests that women fall short of this norm because it is based on male experience, not because women's development is deviant or deficient as some theorists claim. Instead, women develop a different sense of identity and different values based on their fundamental experience of connectedness.

Although Gilligan occasionally writes of the complementarity of the two themes of separation and connection in every life story, she nevertheless insists that the themes characterize two different developmental journeys and necessitate different theories of development. Her primary contention is "that women perceive and construe social reality differently from men" (171) based on their experiences of being rooted in webs of relationships. She concludes:

The failure to see the different reality of women's lives and to hear the differences in their voices stems in part from the assumption that there is a single mode of social experience and interpretation. By positing instead two different modes, we arrive at a more complex rendition of human experience which sees the truth of separation and attachment in the lives of women and men. (173–74)

Gilligan has convinced me not that men and women "perceive and construe social reality differently" (171) but that no "single mode of social experience and interpretation" (173) is normative. Erikson's developmental journey based on separation from others does not reflect the experiences of all men; nor does Gilligan's journey based on attachment to others reflect the experiences of all women. What is important is both theories. What is important is acknowledging different fundamental life experiences that eventuate in different interpretative theories.

Gilligan has also convinced me that both attachment and separation are significant themes in our life stories. For some, the experience of attachment is more fundamental than the experience of separation. For others, the experience of separation is more fundamental than the experience of attachment. These differences have important implications for the homiletical conversation. Traditional homiletical theory presupposes the preacher's separation from the congregation. Some of us need alternative ways of understanding preaching, because the fundamental experience that shapes our sense of the preacher-congregation relationship is that of solidarity, of being inextricably connected within a web of interdependent relationships.

A second voice in this discussion of the alleged gap between the preacher and the congregation is that of Robin West (1988). West locates Gilligan's description of women's connectedness within a more complex grid that reflects a greater variety of human experiences and theoretical interpretations. In addition, West's description of the interplay between subjective experience and theory has helped me understand the staying power of traditional homiletics.

West contends that according to legal and political theorists, the definition of "human being" has been based on a subjectivity of separation. The two dominant legal theories—"liberal legal theory" and "critical legal theory"—are "phenomenological descriptions of the paradigmatically male experience of the inevitability of separation of the self from the rest of the species, and indeed from the rest of the natural world" (5). These two theories "tell a story" or "describe an inner life" that reflects the "subjective experience of masculinity" (5). On the one hand, the "official story," liberal legal theory, celebrates separation as the basis for freedom, equality, and a legal system based on rights. This is "the 'up side' of the subjective experience of separation" (7). The "down side" is a sense of vulnerability and the threat that the "other" poses to the autonomous self. On the other hand, critical legal theory, the unofficial or minority story, reflects the same experience of separation but interprets the experience differently. This "unofficial story" focuses on "a perpetual longing for community, or attachment, or unification, or *connection*" (9, West's italics). These "unofficial" theorists image the autonomous individual as lonely, alienated, and isolated. They describe the fear of isolation and celebrate the collective over the individual. Both theories, West claims, assume that the human being's fundamental existential state is grounded in separation.

The problem, West continues, is that "women's existential state" is grounded in connection (14–15). This is the subjective experience reflected both in cultural feminism, the dominant or "official story" of feminism, and radical feminism, the minority or "unofficial story." Cultural feminism, which Gilligan epitomizes, celebrates women's connectedness with others and propounds a theory based on an ethic of responsibility and care for others. Radical feminism tells a different story: "Invasion and intrusion, rather than intimacy, nurturance and care, is the 'unofficial' story of women's subjective experience of connection" (29). These "unofficial" theorists value and encourage "women's longings for individuation, physical privacy, and independence" (35). Underlying both these versions of feminism is the subjective experience of connection.

West insists that, although autonomy and attachment are "twin desires" of the human condition (51), the fundamental experiences of men and women are different. For men "separation (and therefore autonomy) is what comes naturally," and intimacy is learned (41). While some men value the state of separation, others view it as negative. Unfortunately, "the dominant male culture condemns as aberrant the man who needs others," thereby encouraging men to "deny their need for attachment" (38). For women, connection is what comes naturally, and independence is learned. Some women value the state of connection, whereas others view it as negative. Unfortunately, "the dominant female culture condemns the woman who wants to exist apart from others," thereby encouraging women to "deny their need for individuation" (38).

West concludes that "modern jurisprudence is 'masculine' " (58). Modern jurisprudence, or the Rule of Law, ignores the fundamental experiences that constitute women's lives and thus excludes women and their values (64). Under the Rule of Law, women have essentially been unprotected. West therefore calls on women "to tell the story and phenomenology of the human community's commitment to the Rule of Law from women's point of view" (64), that is, from the underside of those unprotected by the law. She urges women "to flood the market with our own stories until we get one simple point across: men's narrative story and phenomenological description of law is not women's story and phenomenology of law" (56).

If, as West claims, theories are phenomenological descriptions inseparable from subjective experience, then traditional homiletical theory reflects the experience of separation that deeply values love, care for others, and community. Traditional homiletics will continue to be an important voice in the homiletical conversation because it will continue to reflect some preachers' and some congregations' experiences of themselves, the church, the Word of God, and the world. Those of us who understand our lives in the world and in the community of faith to be rooted in connectedness have different stories to tell not only about ourselves, the church, the Word of God, and the world, but also about preaching. As we describe and reflect on our experiences, we will begin to understand more thoroughly what it means to preach and to participate in congregations when "connection and solidarity" (Smith 1989, 48) shape the fundamental relationship between the congregation and the preacher. And we will contribute to the emergence of homiletical theories that are phenomenological descriptions of connectedness.

A third voice from feminist scholarship comes from *Women's Ways of Knowing: The Development of Self, Voice, and Mind* (Belenky and others 1986). Written by four women, *Women's Ways of Knowing* describes five epistemological positions that emerged from extensive interviews with women. All five positions are worth considering briefly as they relate to the roles assigned by traditional homiletical theory to the preacher and the congregation.

In the first two categories, authority figures play a major role. The first "way of knowing" is silence, which results from the unquestioned acceptance of the dictates of authority figures. The women who characterize this position "feel passive, reactive, and dependent" and "see authorities as being all-powerful, if not over-powering" (27). The second epistemological category is knowing through "received knowledge" or through "listening to the voices of others" (35–51). The women characterizing this second position identify themselves as active listeners and as members of a group sharing their exact thoughts and experiences. They sometimes delight in teaching others what they know. Yet these women feel they are unable to "generate facts and ideas through reflection on [their] own experience" (39). They therefore remain dependent on the authority figures to give them truth and right answers. They are convinced that they cannot learn without teachers whose task, in their eyes, is "to pass along [their] knowledge" (40). This mode of teaching and learning educational theorist Paulo Freire terms a "banking" model (214). *Women's Ways of Knowing* summarizes and quotes Freire:

> The teacher's role is "to 'fill' the students by making deposits of information which the teacher considers to constitute true knowledge." The student's job is merely to "store the deposits."[11]

In the banking model of teaching, lectures become "polished products," allowing students to see only the outcome or the result of the teacher's thinking (215). Both silence, category one, and received knowledge, category two, place those in authority in the role of the transmitters of knowledge. Others do not generate knowledge but must receive it from the authority figure.

These first two positions suggest a number of parallels in the field of preaching. My intent is not to equate traditional homiletical theory with the banking model of teaching. Neither is my intent to imply that traditional preaching results in congregational silence or passive dependence on the preacher. These two categories, however, do highlight the fact that silence and dependence represent significant dangers when preachers abuse the position of authority assigned them by traditional homiletical theory. In fact, Cox, one of the foremost proponents of traditional theory, counsels that preaching demands both mutual respect between preachers and congregations and love on the part of preachers for their congregations. What intrigues me here is that these two categories are only two of five, and in no other category is the person of the authority figure prominent. Women and men can come to know in ways other than receiving information from an authority figure.

A third way of knowing results from the rejection of knowledge as truth received from authority figures. *Women's Ways of Knowing* describes this position as subjective knowledge. Truth now becomes "personal, private, and subjectively known or intuited"; it "now resides within the person" (54). The women evidencing this epistemological stance, though often passionate about their own convictions, remain tolerant of others' differing ideas and are unwilling to hurt others' feelings by arguing. Persuading others and "winning arguments" (74) are not their concerns. In addition, they often eschew rationalistic modes of expression, preferring modes that are nonverbal and artistic. Although a valid and important "way of knowing" and an important stage in some women's journey toward self-confidence, subjective knowledge is not the apex of this theory of epistemological development. In fact, it poses its own dangers when all knowledge is equated with private opinions and rational reflection is dismissed as unimportant.

Once again I want to suggest parallels from the perspective of preaching. Preaching based on subjective knowing is not, I believe, a helpful alternative to traditional preaching. The dangers here include that the preacher becomes the proclaimer of a personal or private truth, that the preacher becomes overly concerned with not hurting anyone's feelings, and that preaching focuses solely on being artistic and eschews all rational thinking. Fortunately, two additional categories suggest other ways of knowing and other ways of understanding the task of preaching.

Women's Ways of Knowing labels category four "procedural knowledge" and category five "constructed knowledge." Fundamental to both these categories is the distinction between "separate knowing" and "connected knowing," which the authors posit as "two contrasting epistemological orientations: a separate epistemology, based upon impersonal procedures for establishing truth, and a connected epistemology, in which truth emerges through care" (102).

Before I describe categories four and five in this typology, I will distinguish between these two epistemological orientations. In "separate knowing," the orientation is toward separation between the knower and the object of knowing, a separation that enables the knower to gain mastery over that which is known. The impersonal procedures characteristic of separate knowing include doubting, reasoning, arguing, and extricating oneself, especially one's feelings, from the process of knowing. In addition, those who are separate knowers experience distance between themselves and others with whom knowledge is discussed.

Conversely, in "connected knowing" the orientation is "toward relationship" (101), a relationship that enables the knower to experience intimacy and equality with that which is known. The interpersonal procedures characteristic of connected knowing include talking empathetically with others, sharing small truths, withholding judgment, collaborating, and relying on personal knowledge.

Separate knowing and connected knowing are both fundamental to category four, "procedural knowledge," and to category five, "constructed knowledge." In category four, "procedural knowledge," the two epistemological orientations remain distinct. Procedural knowers are either separate knowers or connected knowers. Their loyalty is to the process by which they came to know and to the external structures that preserve that process. Procedural knowers remain dependent on their roles, institutions, disciplines, or methods for their sense of identity. They remain dependent on their "identification with the power of a group and its agreed-upon ways of knowing" for their sense of authority (134). And they seek satisfaction in "pleasing others or in measuring up to external standards—in being 'the good woman' or 'the good student' or 'the successful woman who has made it in a man's world'" (134).

In "constructed knowledge," category five, the two epistemological orientations, though distinct, become integrated. "Constructivists" can integrate "thinking and feeling" (130), "weaving together the strands of rational and emotive thought" (134). They can shift back and forth between connected knowing and separate knowing. However, these two epistemological orientations in the final analysis are not given equal weight. *Women's Ways of Knowing* gives priority to connected knowledge:

> Among women thinking as constructivists, connected knowing is not simply an "objective" procedure but a way of weaving their passions and intellectual life into some recognizable whole. For women, at least, once they include the self, they use connected "passionate" knowing as the predominant mode for understanding, regardless of whether separate or connected procedures for knowing had been emphasized in the past. (141–42)

These final two categories also suggest a number of parallels with homiletical theory. My intent, once again, is not to suggest that traditional scholars advocate separate knowing to the exclusion of connected knowing. The procedures that characterize separate knowing are not prominent in recent versions of traditional theory. For example, argument, a primary procedure in separate knowing and a major component of Broadus and Weatherspoon's theory of preaching, occupies a modest place, along with other means for developing the sermon, in Cox's theory. And few homiletical scholars, whatever their theory of preaching, require that preachers extricate themselves from the process of sermon preparation and expunge all references to themselves from the sermon. At the same time, traditional homiletics, with its inevitable gap that separates the preacher from the congregation, does envision the preacher as a "separate knower," one with knowledge to impart to the congregation.

In the final analysis, traditional homiletical theory represents a theory of preaching that, while allowing for and valuing connected knowing, is based on separate knowing. The question therefore remains, What is preaching all about for those of us who experience preaching as fundamentally a connected process, albeit encompassing significant amounts of separate knowing? For those of us who identify ourselves as "constructivists" and who give a privileged place to connected knowing, traditional homiletics does not reflect our experiences or emerging understandings of preaching.

Response Two:
The Sermon as Answer

A second problem traditional theory poses for some of us in the church and the academy is its normative power. A number of its claims continue to dominate thinking about what preaching is or ought to be, both in obvious and not so obvious ways.

The persistence of traditional homiletical theory is obvious in the claims that sermons should persuade, inform, give answers, and a host of other verbs that make the preacher the authority figure and imply the one-directional movement of the sermon. I will focus briefly on the claim that sermons should give answers. Raymond E. Brown asserts that in the Roman Catholic Church "we have been emphatic that we have a set of answers and that those need to be repeated and passed on from generation to generation" (1983, 68). Protestant scholars have been equally insistent about the importance of answers: "Concrete human problems, and the Gospel answer, is the best starting-place for sermons."[12] Or again, "people want answers"; "they want to know what is safe to believe and what is the right way to live" (Brokhoff 1985, 13). The normative power of the claim that preaching should provide answers is also found among critics of this view of preaching. Frederick Buechner, for example, describes the pressure that preachers feel to give answers and urges them to resist the temptation (1977, 35–36; see Wilson 1988, 25).

The presupposition that sermons should provide answers is rooted in traditional theory's image of preaching as the transmission of truth from the preacher or through the preacher to the congregation. The suggestion that preaching is not primarily about giving answers, informing, explaining, transmitting, persuading, or communicating a message swims against a powerful current in the homiletical literature.

Other evidence of the persistence and normative power of traditional homiletical theory is less obvious. Richard Eslinger examines five homileticians who, in his estimation, have been most prominent in their efforts to reconstruct homiletical theory (1987). He does not paint a full portrait of the "old homiletic" but characterizes it in two ways. The "old homiletic" is a discursive method of preaching that values sermonic points and propositions (11), and it is an "ideational approach" to preaching (86). Eslinger assumes that his readers are familiar with the literature of homiletical theory and the discursive or ideational approach to preaching found there. My reading of the literature leads me to link Eslinger's "old homiletic," emphasizing propositions or ideas, with what I am calling traditional theory, which envisions the preacher as transmitting or communicating those propositions or ideas to the congregation. What is noteworthy is Eslinger's assessment of the situation in 1987. He claims that, despite efforts to reconstruct homiletical theory, "most of us have tinkered only a bit with the old method" (12).

Further evidence that the "old homiletic," with its concern for propositions and central ideas, is the norm in seminary instruction can be found in a 1984 survey of forms used by teachers of homiletics to evaluate sermons (Wardlaw 1989, 269–311). In that survey, fifteen out of twenty forms asked the evaluators to comment on the central "thought," "idea," "theme," "proposition," "message," or "point" of the sermon. Three additional forms in the survey asked evaluators to assess the sequence of major points or the organization of ideas. Eighteen of twenty forms, then, assume an "ideational approach" to preaching and betray a bias toward the "old homiletic," to use Eslinger's phrases. Those eighteen forms represent eighteen seminaries across the United States and Canada. Thus the fundamental concern of traditional homiletical theory, that a sermon should communicate a message or an idea, continued to reign as of 1984, making the articulation of alternative understandings of preaching difficult.[13]

At the same time that many teachers of preaching remain committed to key tenets of traditional homiletical theory, many students begin their seminary education with traditional images of preaching ingrained in their hearts and minds. For these students the sermon is a message, the preacher is the sender, and the people are passive recipients (Wardlaw 1989, 8). It is no wonder that some of us have found it difficult to resist the normative power of traditional homiletical thinking.

Response Three: The Relationship Between Language and Reality

A third problem, addressed by a few homiletical scholars, focuses on the bond between language and objective reality that traditional homiletics presupposes. The problem arises when the link between words and reality dissolves. In 1965, two scholars wrote nostalgically of a lost linguistic Eden. Otto Semmelroth, quoting philosopher Max Picard, claimed that "the problem of language begins with the fall, when word and thing were torn asunder"; before this fall, "when word and thing were still united, when the word did not denote the thing, but was the thing, and when the thing had a name simply by existing, then there was no problem of language. The word was absorbed in the thing and the thing in the word, each was dissolved in the other."[14]

Helmut Thielicke described the problem similarly:

> Language once adequately expressed a particular relationship to reality, but now when we, whose relationship to reality has changed, use the same words, they become untrue. They cease to be a means of grasping and comprehending reality. (1965, 45)

As a result, for Thielicke contemporary language is sick (44), worn out, and empty (45).

The problem these scholars describe in 1965 persisted fifteen years later. In 1980, James Daane lamented that in much of contemporary life "the nexus between language and reality has been broken and words cut loose from their mooring and cast adrift, so that the meaning of language is up for grabs" (18). From this perspective, "words are not regarded as having rootage in objective realities, but are subject to such meaning as the user sees fit to attribute to them" (19). For Daane, this situation necessitates a rethinking of preaching and its link to divine realities.

Traditional homiletical theory, which assumes that words grasp and convey reality, becomes problematic for these scholars and others of us who see ourselves as living and preaching in a new linguistic situation. For us, confidence in words and their one-to-one correspondence to objective reality, a fundamental presupposition of traditional homiletical theory, is no longer possible. New understandings of language in general and sermonic language in particular enter the homiletical conversation.

Response Four:
An Emphasis on Rationality

A fourth issue that makes traditional theory problematic for some of us is summed up in the charge that it is too rationalistic (Ireson 1958, 29; Wilson-Kastner 1989, 19–20). The rational character of the preaching enterprise is prominent in Broadus and Weatherspoon and continues, though not always as explicitly, in later versions of traditional homiletics. One mark of this rationalistic bent is the insistence that the foremost concern of sermonic language should be clarity. The function of similes and metaphors is to clarify and support the sermon's central message.

Another mark of traditional theory's emphasis on the rational is the subordination of illustration to the more important methods of sermon development—"definition, explanation, restatement, and argument" (Cox 1985, 207). Illustrations—consisting of similes, analogies, metaphors, allegories, anecdotes, parables, and fables—are "supportive" (ibid.) or "auxiliary" (Broadus and Weatherspoon 1944, 196).

Traditional theory's rationalistic bent is also evident in the minor role this theory gives to the imagination and to that which is mysterious or elusive about the preaching enterprise. This bent is evident in discussions of both biblical interpretation and sermon construction. Cox, for example, suggests that, when preachers interpret texts, they should seek to "grasp" the truth and make it "accessible" to others (1985, 61). He recognizes that texts may point to "vast and impenetrable mysteries" before which "we may only stand in wonder," but preachers as interpreters should seek "to make the truth, to whatever degree we can grasp it, accessible to as many of our hearers as possible" (61). Similarly for Cox, designing a sermon is a conscious process. His hope is that preachers will make confident decisions about arranging sermonic material based on "a few dos and don'ts" (140) and a few "basic rules" (130).

Missing here are discussions of the creative power of poetic language, the importance of the preacher's imagination, and the ineffable mystery of God. Traditional theory tends to value the rational and conscious dimensions of preaching more than its imaginative and mysterious dimensions.

The Need for
Other Voices at the Table

Because no single homiletical theory has ever fit all homiletical scholars, pastors, seminarians, or congregations, homiletical theory has always been in flux. Traditional theory remains a major voice in the homiletical conversation not only because it continues to be reshaped to fit the gifts and experiences of contemporary preachers and congregations, but also because many of its central claims remain dominant and normative in other understandings of preaching. While it does not tell the whole story, it is an accurate description of the life experiences and convictions of many believers. The homiletical conversation will be impoverished if traditional homiletics is excluded or disparaged as it continues to shift, broaden, and redescribe its centers and boundaries.

At the same time, traditional theory does not fit all those who preach, who worship within believing communities, who are learning to preach, or who serve as homiletical guides and mentors. Other voices at the homiletical table reflect different experiences and convictions. Since the demise around mid-century of the homiletical consensus revolving around traditional theory, two other major understandings of preaching have emerged. Underlying this emergence of additional voices at the homiletical table are different life experiences, new understandings of the nature of language, and new appreciations of divine mystery and the power of human imagination.

from *Revolutionary Patience*

Dorothee Soelle

He gave answers to questions they didn't ask
sometimes they didn't dare
open their mouths anymore
not because they hadn't understood
he was taking from them
everything sacred and safe
he offered no guarantees
Fire was not sacred to him or neon
not singing or silence
not fornication or chastity
in his speech foxes breaddough
and much mended nets became sacred
the down and out were his proof
and actually he had as much assurance
of victory as we in these parts do

None

2 ∽ *Kerygmatic Theory States Its Claims*

A second major voice in the homiletical conversation shifts its primary indebtedness from John A. Broadus and his dependence on rhetoric to Greek Testament scholar C. H. Dodd and theologian Karl Barth. This second theory of preaching is marked by new emphases on the *kerygma* as the primitive and essential core of the gospel, the Word of God as an active presence in preaching, and the sermon as an event in which God speaks a saving word. I have designated this second theory a kerygmatic understanding of preaching. This second theory both overlaps with traditional theory and breaks new ground. Its heyday was the 1960s, 1970s, and early 1980s.

Listening

Kerygmatic theory deserves attention. Its understanding of the Word of God continues to influence the homiletical conversation today; its discussions of language paved the way for transformational views of preaching; and it remains a distinct, if no longer preeminent, voice at the homiletical table.

Purpose

Kerygmatic homiletical theory describes the purpose of preaching as a both/and: both transmission of the *kerygma* and the event of God's speaking. To traditional theory's emphasis on transmission, this theory adds the eventfulness of the Word.

Dodd contributed to the first half of the both/and, identifying the "original *kerygma*" (1937, 79, 123) that preaching must transmit. Dodd's goal was to extract from the Greek Testament "the actual content of the gospel preached or proclaimed by the apostles" (3) so that modern-day preachers could make "its essential relevance and truth clear" (128).

Barth contributed to the second half of the both/and, identifying the sermon as an event in which God is the true preacher. Barth's preacher is a "herald" (1963b, 16) in whose gospel proclamation "God speaks" (12).

A principal proponent of this understanding of preaching was Robert H. Mounce (1960), and his indebtedness to both Dodd and Barth is evident. Mounce's concern was to address the problem for today's preachers created by the *kerygma* as the content of the apostles' preaching. The *kerygma* provides

the norm for all Christian preaching; yet it comes to twentieth-century preachers in first-century language and concepts. The problem, therefore, is one of
communication, namely, "how effectively to transmit this ancient account of
divine intervention to modern [congregations]" (156). Transmission of the
kerygma, however, is a secondary goal of preaching. Mounce quotes theologian Gustaf Wingren regarding the "single purpose" of preaching—"that Christ
might come to those who have assembled to listen."[1] Mounce describes the
preaching moment:

> When the preacher mounts the pulpit steps he does so under obligation to
> mediate the presence of Almighty God. . . . He must allow *God* to speak. His
> words must bear the Divine Word. His voice must be God's voice. He stands
> before a group of people whose one great need is to be ushered into the
> presence of God. (158)

In actuality, these two facets of preaching's purpose are inseparable for
Mounce: Preaching that communicates the *kerygma* mediates the saving presence of God.

According to Henry H. Mitchell (1979), "Black preaching" is kerygmatic.[2]
On the one hand, he claims, "the implication that God has been speaking has
always been clear" (197). On the other hand, preaching in the Black church
is concerned with "God's truth" (100), "the kerygma" (114), or the gospel,
which "strives for expression" (28). Thus, preaching aims both to facilitate a
"Gospel encounter" (106) and "to give some firm word about God's will for
today" (98).

A kerygmatic understanding of preaching's purpose widens the gap between the preacher and the congregation because of the conviction that in the
sermon God speaks. In some versions of kerygmatic theory, the preacher
speaks for God. Barth recognizes the danger of this claim (1963a, 747). Nevertheless, he quotes Martin Luther:

> A preacher . . . , when he has preached (if he is a true preacher), . . . must
> confess and exult with Jeremiah: Lord, thou knowest that what has gone forth
> from my mouth is right and pleasing to thee. He must boldly say with St.
> Paul and all the apostles and prophets: *Haec dixit dominus,* Thus saith God
> Himself; or, again: In this sermon, I am a confessed apostle and prophet of
> Jesus Christ. . . . For it is not my word but God's, . . . for which He must al-
> ways praise and reward me, saying: You have taught rightly for I have spo-
> ken through you and the Word is mine. Whoever cannot boast thus of his
> preaching repudiates preaching; for he expressly denies and slanders God.[3]

Kerygmatic scholars who follow Barth's lead here elevate the preacher as
God's "mouthpiece" (Jabusch 1980, 15) or "co-worker . . . in the impartation
of eternal salvation" (Mounce 1960, 159). A danger "of this high doctrine of
preaching," according to Clement Welsh, is "mistaking [the preacher's] voice
for God's voice" (1974, 103).

At the same time, Barth also denies preachers the "right to regard [themselves] as set on high" (1963b, 75). Instead, Barth claims, preachers should "love [their] congregation and feel that [they are] one with them," "placing [themselves] on their level" (53).

Similarly, Mitchell claims that the most effective Black preachers "understand and identify with the culture of the Black masses" (1979, 42). This "intimacy" (224) or "close identity" between the preacher and the congregation (103) is of paramount importance in Black preaching:

> Historically, being Black, [the preacher] could not escape having a part in [the congregation's] condition even if he wanted to. Whether he was chosen from the ranks of the membership (as often occurred) or not, there was no social distance. And this is still an essential part of the Black understanding between people and preacher. . . . The Black preacher must be up to his ears in the condition of his people. (104–5)

Mitchell's preacher, however, is also separated from the congregation as "a teacher and mobilizer, a father figure and an enabler," as well as "a celebrant" (210). Although in the Black church "the priesthood of all believers is a fact," "the burden of the priesthood still falls heavily on the Black preacher" (211–12).

Because in kerygmatic theory the gap between the preacher and the congregation always threatens to widen, some kerygmatic scholars insist on dialogue before, during, and after the sermon. Clyde H. Reid, emphasizing the need for dialogue and congregational participation in preaching, warns that a sermon is not likely to become an event if it allows only one-way communication in which one person exerts pressure on another to respond in a certain way (1967, 67). To facilitate dialogue between the preacher and the congregation, Reid suggests pre-sermon Bible study groups and post-sermon discussion groups.

Gene E. Bartlett claims that the active participation of the congregation while a sermon is being preached has not been taken seriously enough (1962, 43). Since preaching's goal is an intimate encounter between the worshiper and God, worshipers are not passive but have an "active part to play": they must open themselves up in their innermost depths to the presence of God (43). Bartlett therefore describes a partnership between the preacher and the congregation (49). He calls on preachers to envision the worshiper in the pew as "a subject acting, not an object acted upon" (44). Then preachers can envision themselves as "engaged not in monologue but in a conversation" (44).

Some scholars who espouse kerygmatic theory follow one tendency in Barth and widen the gap between the preacher and the congregation by elevating the preacher. Other scholars, also following Barth, seek to narrow the gap by describing the preacher's need to stand with the congregation and by emphasizing the importance of the congregation's participation in preaching. In both cases the hope is that as the true gospel is transmitted, God will speak.

Content

In kerygmatic homiletical theory, a both/and describes not only preaching's purpose but also preaching's content, which is both the essential gospel and the saving activity of God. This new description of the what of preaching builds on definitions of the *kerygma,* the Word of God, and revelation that differ from those of traditional homiletics. If the what of preaching in traditional homiletical theory is propositional, objective truth, the what of preaching in this second theory is the *kerygma,* kerygmatic truth, or the gospel's essential kernel, which communicates and effects salvation. Again, Barth and Dodd provide the foundation on which this theory builds.

Dodd's summary of the "primitive *kerygma,*" or the original content of the apostles' preaching, is not a single formula. Sometimes his definition is brief: "The main burden of the *kerygma* is that . . . God has visited and redeemed his people" (1937, 46–47). Sometimes his definition is more lengthy:

> The general scheme of the *kerygma* . . . begins by proclaiming that "this is that which was spoken by the prophets"; the age of fulfillment has dawned, and Christ is its Lord; [the *kerygma*] then proceeds to recall the historical facts, leading up to the resurrection and exaltation of Christ and the promise of his coming in glory; and it ends with the call to repentance and the offer of forgiveness. (72)

Dodd claims that his intent is not to fix the *kerygma* as an irreducible formula (130). His legacy, however, has been just that, a fixed *kerygma.*

Continually acknowledging their indebtedness to Dodd, kerygmatic scholars build their understandings of preaching on the *kerygma* as the essential content of the earliest Christian preaching and thus of all Christian preaching. Roman Catholic scholars who espouse kerygmatic theory identify this *kerygma* as the faith claims of the Roman Catholic Church. Protestant scholars who espouse kerygmatic theory continue to affirm Dodd's formulations or to redefine the *kerygma* by reinterpreting biblical texts and replacing his conclusions. For many Protestant scholars, the specifics of the *kerygma* are continually changing. Yet they agree that a single kernel or core identifies the essential content of Christianity and therefore Christian preaching. For both Roman Catholic and Protestant scholars who espouse kerygmatic theory, the *kerygma* both defines and creates faith; it is both a set of statements and the saving activity of God.

Undergirding this understanding of preaching's content are concepts of the Word of God and revelation inherited from Barth. For Barth, the Word of God is an event; it is the presence of God that one encounters in the Bible. More boldly, Barth claims that "preaching is the Word of God" (1963a, 747): "The Word of God is God Himself in the proclamation of the Church of Jesus Christ" (743). Revelation, like the Word, is also an event—"God's self-offering and self-manifestation" (301) "in and through" Scripture (744) and in preaching (745). At the same time, revelation communicates "information" (30) about God and humanity.

Mounce, as a major Protestant representative of kerygmatic homiletical theory, illustrates how this theory of preaching's content is both similar to and different from traditional theory (1960). Mounce's description of the what of preaching is similar to traditional theory because the *kerygma* can be stated propositionally. Building on and challenging the work of Dodd, Mounce redefines the primitive *kerygma* and encapsulates it in three statements: an assertion regarding the historicity of Jesus' death, resurrection, and exaltation; a theological evaluation of Jesus as Christ and Lord; and an ethical summons to repent and receive forgiveness. While the *kerygma* can thus be stated propositionally, Mounce insists that it is more than these propositions, and here his understanding differs from traditional theory. The *kerygma* is also the medium for God's saving activity (156). The *kerygma* participates in revelation as both "supranatural knowledge concerning the nature and purposes of God" (151) and God's self-disclosure or redemptive activity that believers personally receive (151–53). Therefore, when the *kerygma* is truly preached, God speaks (158–59) and "reveals Himself in redemptive activity" (152).

After Vatican II, some Roman Catholic homiletical scholars began articulating a similar understanding of preaching. One such scholar is Joseph Fichtner (1981). In his descriptions of preaching, the *kerygma*, revelation, and the Word play similar critical roles.

Fichtner begins his discussion of preaching with a discussion of revelation. He claims that prior to Vatican II certain Roman Catholic theologians and pastors, as well as official manuals, identified revelation as a "set of propositions" (4) and "a store of supernatural truths to which faith must give assent" (6). These propositions and truths provided the content for preaching. Fichtner aims to broaden this understanding of preaching's content by basing his discussions of homiletical theory on the view of preaching set forth by Vatican II. This new view of preaching, he claims, combines the Roman Catholic pre–Vatican II tendency to define revelation as a message with the Protestant tendency to define revelation as an event (6).

In line with traditional Roman Catholic thought, Fichtner identifies revelation as a "precious deposit" of knowledge about God and God's relationship to humanity (12). He insists, however, that such knowledge about God is never complete because God is finally mystery.

In line with Protestant thought, Fichtner identifies revelation as an event in which communion with God is established. He equates revelation with "God's self-manifestation, self-disclosure, even self-communication" (4), and the "*what* of revelation, namely, its content . . . is *God*" (12). Because Fichtner's preacher is "a revealer" and "a transmitter of divine revelation" (16), preaching's content is identical with that of revelation, both God and knowledge of God.

This content of preaching Fichtner links with the *kerygma*. As the apostolic message of salvation, the *kerygma* is valid "for all time" and "sets the norm and goal of the whole preaching of the Church" (81). Once again, however, the *kerygma* is both a message and an event: "The revelation the kerygma hands down is not and cannot be a pure communication of an intellectual message, commanding an intellectual assent, but an event that brings salvation and sanctification" (91).

Playing a similar role in Fichtner's understanding of preaching's content is the concept of the Word of God. Like the *kerygma,* the Word of God both communicates "news about God" and is active in generating faith (40).

For Fichtner, these two halves of preaching's content—truth about God and God's saving presence (12)—are inseparable: "The word of proclamation contains 'the word of life' and hands it on; it makes Jesus and his gift of salvation present; it actually communicates the proclaimed reality to the believer" (15–16).

An important claim for the *kerygma* in kerygmatic views of preaching deserves further discussion. The claim is that the *kerygma,* or the core of the gospel, cannot change. Scholar after scholar makes this claim. Four examples will suffice.

W. Norman Pittenger insists that "the Christian gospel, the *kerygma* or proclamation, indeed remains and must remain fixed as the message of the Church, the heart of its life and the meaning of its existence" (1962, 12).

Claude H. Thompson affirms with equal certainty: "By now the theme of the *kerygma* is familiar to readers of modern theology. There seems to be an irreducible core of New Testament preaching which may neither be ignored nor diminished lest the Christian message be destroyed" (1962, 1–2).

Colin Morris, like a number of Protestant kerygmatic scholars, defers to Dodd, who "distilled the essence of the Gospel of the primitive Church into a series of deceptively simple statements" (1975, 151–52). Morris summarizes Dodd's *kerygma* in 102 words and then exclaims, "That's it—the Christian Faith in a nutshell. That is all which needs to be said" (152).

Willard Francis Jabusch, after introducing Barth's image of the preacher as an ancient herald, insists that "it was . . . very clear to every herald that he was in no way to modify, subtract, or add anything to the message" (1980, 15–16).

The content of kerygmatic preaching is the *kerygma,* the unchangeable heart of the Christian gospel. Its eventfulness makes preaching eventful, and this eventfulness distinguishes kerygmatic understandings of preaching from traditional understandings.

Language

Two key assumptions about language undergird this second theory of preaching. Unlike traditional theory, where discussions of language are limited to sermonic language, in kerygmatic theory the discussions broaden to include concerns about the nature of language in general.

The first assumption is that the preacher's words mediate God's Word so that a sermon mediates God's saving activity. Several similarities with traditional theory and several differences are noteworthy here.

The assumption that sermonic words mediate God's Word continues the link, made in traditional theory, between preaching and communication. The emphasis in kerygmatic theory, however, shifts from the preacher as communicator to God as communicator. God is responsible for communicating to worshipers the saving Word as self-revelation. Some scholars absolve the preacher of all responsibility for shaping the sermon into effective communication. These scholars claim that the preacher must simply preach the unadorned gospel and leave the results to God. God as the true preacher makes the sermon's words persuasive and effective.

This assumption that human words communicate God's Word also rests on another similarity with traditional theory—the positing of a reality that exists apart from language. The difference between the two theories is that in kerygmatic theory the *kerygma,* or God's Word as divine self-revelation, is the link with or the mediator of divine reality, whereas in traditional theory the assumption is that all words are capable of conveying the reality to which they point.

Several kerygmatic homiletical scholars no longer believe traditional theory's presupposition that a bond joins words and the reality to which they refer. For these scholars, the bond has been severed. Thus, a kerygmatic understanding of preaching becomes their answer to this problem of language.

One such scholar is Otto Semmelroth, who proposes that the fallen condition of language is overcome in part by "God's self-communication in grace through the word of preaching" (1965, 246). His focus is "the healing power of Christ's redemption," which "has, to a great extent, restored to the word its union with the thing" (246). A "divine guarantee" preserves the word of preaching from error (175). Thus, although words in general may no longer correspond to reality, God reconnects the word of preaching to divine reality so that preaching is effective.

In a similar fashion, James Daane acknowledges the contemporary claim of language that words have no "rootage in objective realities" (1980, 19). But he contends that such a claim does not hold for preaching. To understand preaching, he argues, one must recover the biblical understanding of the Word of God as active in preaching to accomplish God's will. Daane describes the Word of God as "evocative, dynamic, creative, saving, sin-annulling, death-defeating, healing, life-giving" (29). He urges preachers to believe that a sermon is "a unique mode of address" (46) because in a sermon God speaks a converting, saving Word (8–15, 42). The preacher's task is not to ensure that the sermon is effective, but to preach the gospel message, adding nothing to "the content of the sermonic Word" (47) and trusting that "the Word of God is powerful enough to work its own way through the resistance of the human heart to achieve its saving purpose" (44).

Although only a few kerygmatic scholars discuss the claim that language in general is fallen, a number of them base their views of preaching on the belief that the proclamation of the gospel becomes effective because God's Word speaks through the sermon's words. The sermon's words "become vehicles for the offering and receiving of Christ" (Ward 1958, 46); they "convey the Divine Word" (Mounce 1960, 159). Or again, although the sermon's words are always inadequate, they became "eventful" because "God comes to our rescue and turns preaching into an act of revelation" (Morris 1975, 35). Underlying these schol- ars' statements is Barth's claim, "God speaks through our words" (1963b, 14).

This first assumption about sermonic language is that human words com- municate God's Word. The understanding that the Word of God is the active power of God speaking through the preacher's words is a major legacy of kerygmatic theory in the homiletical conversation today, where it continues to play a significant role.

A second linguistic assumption undergirds kerygmatic homiletical theory— that words and the reality to which they refer are separable so that, although reality does not change, language does and should. This assumption also evi- dences a similarity to and difference from traditional homiletical theory. The *kerygma,* the content of preaching in kerygmatic homiletical theory, is like truth, the content of preaching in traditional homiletics. Both have a reality apart from human experience and perception. And both can be drawn from the Bible, stated succinctly, and offered to others in preaching. Thus, like truth, the *kerygma* is objective and propositional. The difference is that in kerygmatic homiletical theory reality and language can be separated: the *kerygma* is un- changeable, but the words that attempt to describe it are constantly changing. This linguistic assumption brings to the foreground a problem that is not em- phasized in traditional theory: the Bible presents the *kerygma* in first-century language. A critical task facing the preacher becomes translating the biblical formulations of the *kerygma* into modern terminology.

The problem of translation is evident in Dodd. Contemporary preachers must preach in a way that is faithful to "the primitive formulation of the gospel" (1937, 127); they must not preach "another gospel" (128). Yet this *kerygma,* because of its "primitive formulation," is "alien, . . . completely out of touch . . . with our ways of thought" (127). Therefore, like "the great thinkers of the New Testament period," contemporary preachers must restate the gospel in "bold, even daring, ways" (128).

Both these concerns—to preserve the *kerygma* unchanged and to restate it for contemporary believers—are of particular interest to Mounce (1960). His analysis of preaching in the Greek Testament leads him to Dodd's conclusion about a single *kerygma.* Contemporary preaching must proclaim this same *kerygma* in language that the congregation can understand, just as "John and the author of Hebrews restated Biblical concepts in terms that were meaning- ful to their ever-widening audience" (156–57). Mounce therefore endorses the "crusade for linguistic renovation" with one caveat: He insists that any attempt to modernize religious language must ensure that "such modernization actu- ally clarifies the basic message and does not subtly turn it into something that it was never meant to be" (157). The preacher's task is to proclaim the un-changing message of salvation "with utmost clarity" (157). And God's task is "the effective communication of that message" (157). Any problem of com-munication is not that the *kerygma* is difficult for the contemporary world to understand, but that humanity is unwilling to be open to God, for "God speaks, but man stuffs his fingers into his ears" (157). Mounce's view of the language of preaching shares with traditional homiletics the emphasis on clarity of ex-pression. Although translating is a necessity, his chief concern is for the ser-mon's words accurately to communicate the biblical *kerygma* so that the ser-mon becomes a saving event.

Unlike Mounce, other scholars who espouse kerygmatic views of preach-ing emphasize the need for imagination in the tasks of translating and pro-claiming the *kerygma*. W. Norman Pittenger describes "a great theological re-vival" of his day (1962, 19) that concerned theological jargon, biblical language, and the need for translation. Like Mounce, Pittenger's caveat is that it must be the gospel "that we are translating, and not some bright and novel ideas of our own" (20). Unlike Mounce, however, Pittenger claims that the dif-ficulty in communicating the gospel is not solely "the sinfulness" of the con-gregation (20). For Pittenger, the problem is that the language and the patterns in which preachers talk are unrelated to the world in which the members of the congregation live (20). The need, Pittenger claims, is for "new ways of ex-pression" (21). While the *kerygma* must remain "true to the abiding affirma-tion of faith which gives the Church its essential being" (17), it comes in the language of story, symbol, and poetry (12). This imaginative language, which is metaphorical and evocative, Pittenger contrasts with language that is literal, scientific, or philosophical (12–13). Those who speak about God must use imaginative language because "we *cannot* speak literally about God and his ways, as if we had a precise chart for the purpose of mapping the divine ac-tivity" (14). Following Thomas Aquinas, Pittenger claims that theological lan-guage, and thus "language appropriate to the gospel," is metaphorical lan-guage, the language of likeness, not identity: "We speak, and can only speak, in metaphor" (14). The *kerygma,* therefore, because its original form is metaphor and story, demands to be translated (17). The task of preaching is finding new, metaphorical words for the old, unchangeable gospel.

Describing Black preaching, Henry H. Mitchell similarly writes both about the *kerygma* (1979, 114), or "eternal truth," (113) and the need for translation. He claims that "the chief task of hermeneutics is to convey the revelation in its contemporary context" (25). Hermeneutics is about translating, "putting the gospel on a tell-it-like-it-is, nitty-gritty basis" (30). Such translating involves stating "the gospel in the language and culture of the people—the vernacular" (29). Thus the Black preacher "must be fluent in Black language" (152). At its best, translation also requires use of the imagination (121) as well as a "fresh style and vibrancy" (26).

In discussing the use of "the Black imagination" in preaching (136), Mitchell asks a critical question implied by both Mounce and Pittenger: "How can one be sure [the preacher] is not changing or outright destroying God's message?" (137). For Mitchell, the three answers "are easy" (138). First, the preacher should maintain "technical faithfulness to the original account" (138). Second, augmentation should resemble "reconstitution" as though the biblical version were "dried milk or dehydrated soup" (138). Third, the gospel "implies proclamation, interpretation or hermeneutic, and understanding in depth" (139). Mitchell's concern, like that of Mounce and Pittenger, is to preserve the gospel from distortion while still relating it to contemporary life (25, 29).

In discussing this task of translation, a few scholars use the image of dress. Jesse Jai McNeil, like Pittenger and Mitchell, stresses the importance of the imagination in reinterpreting biblical concepts and doctrines. He warns:

> In making such concepts and doctrines intelligible and attractive, the preacher-prophet must be careful not to divest them of their Biblical content, but he must dress them in clothes suitable for a proper introduction to persons whom they should impress upon their first meeting and whose commitment they are to gain. (1961, 96–97)

For McNeil, sermonic language must convey biblical content both accurately and attractively. Similarly, Stephen C. Doyle insists that the gospel must be "unclothed from the language and thought patterns of a distant and alien world" so that it may "take on the clothing of the present" (1982, 22).

Other scholars who do not explicitly use the image of dress presuppose that words can and must change, whereas kerygmatic content can and must remain unchanged. James W. Clarke claims that the preacher should "express the revelation in his own words and manner, but he cannot and dare not change its meaning" (1960, 20).

Two linguistic assumptions characterize kerygmatic understandings of preaching. One assumption is that the sermon's words mediate God's saving Word. The other assumption is that words and reality are separable so that reality is constant, whereas words change. Consequently, the *kerygma* does not and must not change, even while it can and must be translated into contemporary terms.

A major legacy of kerygmatic theory that continues to influence contemporary discussions of preaching is the image of the Word of God as active in the sermon, making it a dynamic event. A second legacy involves the importance of the imagination, metaphoric language, and story in many discussions of translation by kerygmatic scholars. These legacies move the conversation at the homiletical table in the new directions.

Form

In terms of purpose, content, and language, kerygmatic homiletical theory represents a significant broadening of, and sometimes a break with, traditional theory. Discussions of form by kerygmatic scholars evidence little that is different from similar discussions by traditional scholars.

The only new element in kerygmatic theory is the insistence by some scholars on a correspondence between the shape of the text and the shape of the sermon. This insistence is characteristic of Barth, who describes "the preacher of the Gospel" as "guided by the text, not by a topic" (1963b, 81). A sermon's form should follow the text's rhythm and observe its proportions (81), proceeding "verse by verse," except when verses vary in quality and emphasis (81). Barth's rule for sermonic form is that "the essential content of the text must govern the development" (81).

Several kerygmatic scholars reflect this understanding of form and at times distinguish their claim from that of traditional theory. Jean-Jacques von Allmen insists that the text, not "laws of oratory," must guide sermon construction (1962, 54). Ronald E. Sleeth distinguishes between biblical sermons, which he prefers, and rational sermons with an outline and points that are not derived from the text (1964, 39). Mitchell identifies a preference among Black preachers for "Bible stories" (1979, 141) and suggests that this preference is reflected in their choice of sermonic form: "There is probably a higher percentage of sermons preached by Blacks in which the whole outline consists of the telling, at length, of a Bible story" (178). This concern for the text as the guide to sermonic form characterizes a limited number of scholars who advocate kerygmatic homiletical theory.

A concern more universally shared by kerygmatic homiletical scholars continues a basic tenet of traditional theory. Daane, who contends that the form of the sermon should be "determined solely by the text" (1980, 66), describes [the] "one basic rule to which any type of sermon structure must yield tribute. *Every sermon must say one thing, and one thing only; and this one thing must be capable of statement in a single sentence*" (1980, 58, Daane's italics). In a discussion that echoes traditional theory, Daane identifies this single sentence as the sermon's proposition that derives from the biblical text, governs the construction of the sermon, and should be reaffirmed in the conclusion. Other kerygmatic homiletical scholars emphasize the importance of stating "the truth of the Scripture in one sentence" before the preacher turns to sermon construction (Brown, Clinard, and Northcutt 1963, viii). Edward F. Markquart links this emphasis on the sermon's having a single focus with preaching's goal as transmission:

> [H. Grady] Davis and every other author talk about the importance of designing a sermon around one major theme, trunk, magnetic field, or thread.
> . . . Sermons usually need to have one fundamental assertion/theme/truth/message which is reinforced by story, illustration, anecdote, parable, and quotation—all serving to visualize that one fundamental motif. As many preachers were taught: "Better to drive home one point than to leave three stranded on base." (1985, 28)

Singularity of focus serves the same purpose in kerygmatic theory as in traditional theory: If the preacher is clear about the message being sent, the congregation is more apt to receive that message accurately.

Another similarity between discussions of form by kerygmatic homiletical scholars and traditional scholars involves the purpose of story-sermons. Markquart claims that stories express truth, and the story-sermon "helps it slip through the ears and into the mind and heart" (1985, 141). For Mitchell, preachers who retell the biblical narrative should use their imaginations in order "to breathe life into both the story and the truth it teaches" (1979, 121). Thus, kerygmatic homiletical theory follows traditional theory; the story-sermon is a strategy for communicating the sermon's message.

The larger context for this understanding of story-sermons is a particular presupposition about art and parallels between art and preaching. Daane begins his discussion of sermonic form by pointing out similarities between the artist and the preacher. Artists, he contends, may bend the rules of construction, but, if they are "to communicate something to others," they cannot disregard all the rules (1980, 58). He continues: "Every kind of artist must defer to the demands imposed by the message or idea to which he or she seeks to give artistic expression" (58). Similarly, Mitchell compares the Black preacher and the playwright: each "has a message" (1979, 133). In addition, for Daane both art and preaching are about the communication of a message or an idea. And both art and preaching presuppose a sequence: first get the message or idea and then find a form to express it.

In terms of sermon construction, except for those scholars who identify the text as the guide for sermonic form, kerygmatic homiletical theory represents nothing new. Because of its emphasis on preaching as the transmission of the gospel, rules for sermon construction that hold for traditional preaching continue to hold.

Responding

Kerygmatic homiletical theory makes a significant contribution to the homiletical conversation. It adds to traditional theory's understanding of preaching as persuasive discourse the understanding of preaching as eventful discourse. This image of the sermon as event recognizes what worshipers sometimes experience while a sermon is being preached. Kerygmatic homiletical theory also gives a more dominant role to God's presence in preaching through the activity of the Word, an emphasis that continues in much of the homiletical scholarship today. The shift in focus from the preacher to God was important for me, as a woman, when I was learning to preach in the early 1970s. At that time, when most preachers were men, the image of God as the true preacher took the spotlight off me and my discomfort in the pulpit and turned the spotlight on God. I could envision myself preaching not because of what I might bring to preaching but because of what God would bring, that is, God's active, redemptive presence. Finally, some scholars with a kerygmatic understanding of preaching resist the widening gap between the pulpit and the pew and begin to emphasize the need for preaching to be a two-directional process, a dialogue between the preacher and the congregation. However, several problems remain and several new problems arise. Five issues demand attention.

Response One: The Gap
Between Preacher and Congregation

The first issue is that the gap remains; thus the roles assigned by kerygmatic theory have not essentially changed from those assigned by traditional theory. The preacher who seeks to transmit to the worshipers the essential gospel continues to stand apart from them as the authority figure who brings the correct formulation or reformulation of the *kerygma,* or gospel.

Kerygmatic homiletical theory also leaves the role of the congregation essentially unchanged. The worshipers are potentially more active in the sermonic process through pre-sermon and post-sermon discussion groups and during the sermon as they open themselves to God's presence. Yet they remain in the position of receiving the sermon's message from or through the preacher. The purpose of the discussion groups, as described in the literature, is to enable the preacher to compose the sermon in such a way that the congregation will more readily accept its message as truth and thereby experience the sermon as a saving encounter. The congregation thus remains the "target" of the sermon (Semmelroth 1965, 72–73; Horne 1983, 10).

Some kerygmatic homiletical scholars try to ease the gap between the pulpit and the pew; others reinforce the essential one-directional nature of preaching and the authority of the preacher and thereby intensify the gap. Yet, whether the gap is eased or intensified, it remains and prevents kerygmatic theory from describing experiences of preaching that are rooted in a sense of solidarity between the preacher and the congregation.

Response Two:
Preaching as Event

A second problem haunts kerygmatic homiletical theory: Its insistence that every sermon should be an event is too grand. Two descriptions of preaching attest to the grandeur of these expectations. First:

> The aim and purpose of preaching is now, I hope, clear. The preacher tries to bring about a personal encounter between God and the souls of his hearers. He seeks to lead every man to a place where he must meet God face to face. (Tizard 1958, 18)

Second, "A wholesome sermon should leave the hearers in the position of the disciples on the Mount of Transfiguration, face to face with Jesus only" (Wright 1958, 12).

Bartlett is more modest about the sermon's being an event and speaks of those "times when nothing seems to be happening in the affairs of faith" (1962, 98). For him, a sermon is not always an event, but "holds the promise of being the saving Event of Christ" (59). In those times when nothing seems to happen, the sermon offers "an expectancy, a looking forward with hope, a sustaining belief that in the fullness of time the door will open" (98).

Other scholars have also raised the issue of the high expectations of preaching as event. Markquart voices the skepticism of some:

> It is often difficult for us preachers to believe that our voices are the living voice of God on Sunday morning, knowing how capable we are of banality and boredom, insipidity and shallowness (these are the recurring words used by writers on homiletics to describe the average preaching in America). It is hard to believe that God's voice can be so banal and boring, so insipid and shallow, so . . . human. (1985, 85)

Markquart's answer is to restate the convictions of preaching as event. He reiterates, "Through the living voices of common and ordinary men and women . . . we hear the voice of the living God" (85).

Similarly, Sleeth recognizes that some people have difficulty with preaching because "it is not effective communication—not dialogic enough, too rationalistic, too authoritarian" (1986, 5). Sleeth then suggests that these are not the real reasons for their difficulty with preaching. He suggests that perhaps "the real reason" is "that they no longer believe a Word has come to them"; perhaps they "wonder if anything or anyone is 'coming through'"; perhaps they "no longer feel that God has 'spoken' or is 'speaking'" (5). Like Markquart, Sleeth does not question his theory of preaching or entertain the possibility that the image of every sermon as a saving event might be too grand an image. Instead, like Markquart, he restates the claims of kerygmatic homiletical theory—that preaching is "God's coming" (24), "a medium of God's Presence" (25), a saving event that happens again and again (6).

These homiletical scholars admit that problems accompany the claim that every sermon should be an event.[4] Yet their responses simply reaffirm the basic conviction of kerygmatic theory—that every sermon should and can become an encounter between the congregation and God's saving Word. But perhaps sermons only occasionally become saving events. Perhaps something else is happening in those seasons "when nothing seems to be happening in the affairs of faith" (Bartlett 1962, 98).

Response Three: The Individual
Versus the Community

A third issue regarding kerygmatic homiletical theory is its focus on the individual worshiper. The preacher should aim "to bring about a personal encounter between the individual soul and God" (Tizard 1958, 79). Or "a sermon

is an event . . . through which God may speak his Word to the individual worshiper" (Read 1988, 33). This focus on the individual reflects perhaps an additional instance of the influence of Dodd on kerygmatic homiletical theory.
Dodd wrote, "The preaching of the Church is directed towards reconstituting
in the experience of individuals the hour of decision which Jesus brought."[5]

Although this emphasis on the individual worshiper is dominant in kerygmatic homiletical theory, in Barth and a few kerygmatic homiletical scholars,
it is balanced by an understanding of the individual's relationship to the believing community.

For Barth, the community of faith is responsible for hearing and receiving
the Word of God. He claims:

> The Word of God is not spoken to individuals, but to the Church of God and
> to individuals only in the Church. The Word of God itself, therefore, demands
> this community of hearing and receiving. Those who really hear and receive
> it do so in this community. They would not hear and receive it if they tried
> to withdraw from this community. (1963a, 588)

This communal hearing and receiving results in "the common proclamation of
the Word of God . . . which is the task laid upon the Church" (591, see 757).
The commission to all church members "to share in God's own work of proclaiming His Word" (575) is grounded in baptism (744) and in the Word "entrusted" to the church (746).

Although Semmelroth argues that preaching should be directed to the indi-
vidual, he also argues like Barth that the individual can hear and follow God's
Word only within the fellowship of God's people, the church (1965). God's
Word "is not issued separately to many isolated individuals, but socially. . . .
God's word speaks in history to the community of the people of Israel. . . .
The reason the word is addressed to the people however is that it may sum-
mon the individual within this fellowship to decision" (81–82). The personal
decision, in turn, draws the individual into "participation in the redemptive
drama of the people of God" (184). The individual is thus inseparable from the
community, and the community, inseparable from the individual. God's activity is concerned with both the church and the individual and cannot affect the
one without affecting the other (184).

Another kerygmatic scholar who emphasizes the importance of the community is Rudolf Bohren (1965). Like Barth and Semmelroth, Bohren places
the individual believer within the community. He writes, "There can be no
communion with the Spirit, no hearing of the Word, without communion in a
concrete congregation" (105). For Bohren, of critical importance are these
facts: "that the Spirit is promised to the community, that I cannot walk in the
Spirit as an individual with the aid of my free spiritual life or my inner light
or my decision, but only as a member of the community, . . . that persever-
ance implies being surrounded by the charismatic community" (105). In this

context, preaching both proclaims the Christ who "lives" and "works in the community" and equips the community for the communal task of "being a pastor" (131). This task of "being a pastor" involves mutual edification and support (132). Preaching therefore upbuilds the congregation as an ongoing, interactive community. In turn, "solidarity" within the community becomes "a paradigm for solidarity with the world" and with creation (128).

A problem with kerygmatic theory is its overwhelming emphasis on the individual worshiper and the personal encounter that constitutes the sermonic event. A few homiletical scholars like Semmelroth and Bohren begin to shift this emphasis and place the individual within the community of faith. This shift in focus raises new questions: What would homiletical theory look like that gives priority to the Word entrusted to the community? What would homiletical theory look like that focuses on the preacher as a "community builder" (Doyle 1982, 88) and on the congregation not as a collection of individuals but as a community of faith within the world and creation? These questions challenge homiletical theory to explore new directions.

Response Four:
An Unchanging *Kerygma*

A fourth problem that kerygmatic theory raises for some homiletical scholars focuses on claims to certainty that accompany formulations of the essential gospel message, the *kerygma,* or the Word of God, to be preached. Kerygmatic scholars presuppose that the gospel, the Word, or the *kerygma* is fixed and "obvious" (Wright 1958, 25). But other scholars are not so certain. James T. Cleland raises the issue. He begins *Preaching to Be Understood* (1965) with a summary of four nineteenth-century sermons that attempt to interpret President Lincoln's assassination. Each sermon has a different emphasis: one on revenge, a second on "the sin of hero worship," a third on "the Good-Friday martyr," and a fourth on "gentle agnosticism" (14). Then Cleland poses a series of questions:

> Do you sense the problem? What is the Word of God on such an occasion? On any occasion? What is the gospel, the good news? What is the norm by which a minister judges what he, under God, preaches? What is his point of reference, the polestar by which he steers himself and his folk? Were all four emphases in the Lincoln sermons valid interpretations of the Word of God? Why? Why not? Where does a minister turn so as to find what God says for the contemporary scene? (14).

Cleland's answer is what he calls the "unambiguous, central, recurring fact upon which the Bible and Jesus and the Holy Spirit and the tradition fundamentally agree" (28). His answer is his personal formulation of the *kerygma,* preaching's "norm," which goes "something like this": "God of his own free will is constantly seeking to bring man into right relations with him, not because of any merit on man's part, but because of God's own nature" (28). Cleland refuses to let go of his confidence in the ability of the *kerygma* to be clearly articulated. He raises a critical problem and then returns to a formulaic answer.

Alvin J. Porteous likewise believes in the existence of "the essentials of the Christian message" (1979, 35), but his formulation of this message challenges Cleland's. For Porteous, the biblical message is a word of liberation. The church's "social and economic conditioning" as a privileged group of people has resulted in an "ideological skewing of [its] message" (34). Consequently, the church is "faced with the difficult task of disentangling the message of the gospel from these ideological accretions and distortions" (36). Porteous aims to articulate a liberating formulation of the essential gospel. His hope is that, if the preacher gets the message right, the sermon will once again become a "liberating event" (60). Porteous is sure that an undistorted message of the gospel can be recovered and preached. He is equally sure that the message of the privileged church is distorted.

Cleland's and Porteous's discussions of the gospel's essence raise an important question, Who defines the *kerygma?* According to Porteous, Cleland's formulation of the gospel is ideologically skewed because it represents the perspective of the privileged church and ignores the socially and economically liberating dimensions of the gospel. For centuries the privileged and the powerful have defined the *kerygma.* Justo L. González and Catherine Gunsalus González tell the story of how Christian doctrine became coopted by "the views and interests of the powerful" (1980, 15). The interpretation of the Christian faith by the powerful "became normative and was passed on as authoritative, not only to later generations among the powerful, but also to the powerless, who were left with the alternative of either acquiescing to exploitation or rejecting Christianity" (15). González and González, like Porteous, suggest that the gospel is best understood by those who are powerless and oppressed (16–19). So the question, Who defines the *kerygma?* is a critical one, and the gospel's core is defined differently depending on who is allowed to contribute to the definition.

Does an unchanging *kerygma* exist? While some scholars, like Porteous, continue to answer "Yes" and seek to reformulate its message, other scholars question whether an undistorted formulation of the gospel is possible. William J. Hill suggests that in the Bible the *kerygma* "does not confront us with one monolithic meaning that needs only to be transferred unchanged into the present, as objectively a finished product that needs but to be translated into contemporary idiom, or updated into today's cultural ambiance" (1983, 114).

As though responding to Hill's claim that the Bible offers no single *kerygma,* Ernest Best asks, "But does not the New Testament . . . provide ways of stating the central kerygma of the faith?" (1988, 26). Best answers his own question with claims similar to Hill's: The Greek Testament reflects different

emphases (26) and understandings of Christian faith (28–29), as well as con-
tradictory views (32). The only absolute, Best concludes, is Jesus Christ the
Word, not facts about him extracted from Scripture, not some "fixed, final, and
irreducible interpretation of the significance" (31).

A very subtle distinction separates Hill and Best. Hill posits a break between
the *kerygma* as a divine reality and words that attempt to express it; Best posits
a break between the *kerygma* as a human reality—those "fixed, final, and irreducible" formulations (ibid.)—and divine reality. In either case, the gulf between words and the divine reality to which they refer reappears. Hill and Best
are among those scholars who are no longer convinced that the *kerygma,* the
gospel, or the Word of God, is an unchanging, discernible message that can
be formulated with absolute certainty.

For some homiletical scholars, certainty in matters of faith gives way to uncertainty. Whereas most scholars assume that truth can be known with some
degree of assurance, other scholars discard the need for certainty. Joseph Sittler finds "something humorous" in the supposition that one can "pull a single
magic lever and open a jangling jackpot of certainty" (1966, 25–26). Welsh describes "an uncertainty that is never to be removed" (1974, 43). John Claypool
narrates the event that "marked the end of innocence for me" regarding "religious certainty" (1980, 92). D. W. Cleverley Ford declares, "All certainties are
dead certainties" (1979, 14). And Paul Scherer counsels that "we have to be
content in the matter of our Christian faith with something other than the kind
of certainty which so many seem to covet—lest our faith turn into knowledge
considerably ahead of schedule" (1965, 28).

One of the underlying issues here involves the status of knowledge. Bartlett
believes that reality is knowable. He describes the scientist as one who "by
limiting the area of his investigation and submitting himself to the discipline
of the scientific method, . . . can come to a pragmatic knowledge of an area
of reality. Our scientific age is clear evidence that he has fulfilled his claim to
an amazing degree" (1962, 18). Bartlett then describes the preacher as one who
"can enter into the knowledge, not of a limited area of reality, but of God, the
ground of all reality" (18–19).

Sittler, however, believes differently. He writes that even scientists "no
longer talk of knowledge as if that term promised statements or formulas corresponding to the nature of things" (1966, 51). He explains his understanding
of this changed situation:

> For four hundred years the Western world has really believed that empirical
> investigation could unfold and disclose and bring into intelligible statement
> the nature of things. This faith is dead—not in the thought of the common
> life which still idolizes this procedure and hope as if it were sound, but dead
> in the judgment of its most advance[d] practitioners. (51)

This changed situation regarding the status of knowledge is linked for Sittler
to a linguistic problem, which is "the unique problem of the second half of this

century: the discovery that there is no necessary correspondence between the grammar of our beholding minds and the nature of things" (51). Knowledge is not a clear reflection of reality because language is not automatically a clear reflection of reality. Consequently, knowing is no longer a simple activity, produced by the correct philosophical, scientific, or exegetical method. Instead, Sittler claims, "the ways of knowing must be as supple and contrapuntal and various as history is—not as clear and clean and simple as philosophy hungers for" (26).

Kerygmatic homiletical theory becomes a problem for those of us who are no longer certain that language, even biblical language, reflects divine reality without distortion. For us new questions arise: What is the content of preaching in the absence of an unchanging, self-evident *kerygma?* What happens in preaching if language does not grasp reality, including divine reality? These questions push toward different understandings of what preaching is all about.

Response Five: The Complexity of Language and Translating

A fifth issue that kerygmatic homiletical theory raises involves the task of translation. This issue is particularly highlighted by the image of changing clothes. At stake is the presupposition that words are interchangeable. If words are instead slippery, without clear significations, and if therefore words are not substitutable, then the task of translating demands rethinking.

Like McNeil and Doyle, Karl Rahner conceives of the gospel as "clothed" in biblical concepts and images (1968, 21) and claims that, for the sermon's message to be "transmitted" (24), the preacher must translate the Christian message as accurately as possible (24–38). Unlike McNeil and Doyle, however, he discusses the profound complexity of the task of translating the gospel.

In the first place, Rahner recognizes that the meanings of words shift. Language is "constantly changing," "never the same for any two people" (23). A particular word, far from having a simple definition, is "wrapped in various associated meanings, feelings and experiences" (23). Furthermore:

> No "definition" of a word is final; one defines with other words which should be defined in turn. But definition is then no longer possible because one cannot go on indefinitely, and it is totally untrue that there are words which can be absolutely clear *in themselves* and need no further explanation. Therefore, we have to be reconciled to a language which is not subject to conscious control and, though apparently precise, is in reality obscure. We must rely on the way in which words are used in spite of their limitations. (23–24)

Thus for Rahner, translation is difficult because defining words is no simple task.

In the second place, Rahner recognizes the inevitable linguistic nature of thinking; no thought exists apart from words (1964, 3). Words are not "external façades behind . . . which lives simply one and the same thought" (4).

Words therefore are not interchangeable (4). Rahner suggests an analogy: one cannot take a soul, give it a new body, and expect the body to remain unchanged (4).

In the final analysis, Rahner believes that the "real meaning" of "the old formulae of Scripture and tradition" can be translated (1968, 27) and that the "enduring message" can be carried over "from the language of one age to that of another age" (23). Yet the process is "very complex" because of the complexity of language (23).

Ernest Best complicates the task of translation even further (1988, 33–53) and concludes that translation is not possible; to translate the gospel is to transmute it (53). For Best, "there is no biblical theology" (52) capable of producing a reliable formulation of the gospel which then requires translation. One finds in the Bible instead biblical theologies (52). Finally, for Best, the task is not translation of discerned truth but interpretation of biblical texts (53).

This final issue paves the way for new understandings of preaching. New insights into the complexity of language and a shift from extracting and translating an unchanging gospel to interpreting texts push homiletical thinking toward different descriptions of why, what, and how we preach.

It is Dangerous to
Read Newspapers

Margaret Atwood

While I was building neat
castles in the sandbox,
the hasty pits were
filling with bulldozed corpses

and as I walked to the school
washed and combed, my feet
stepping on the cracks in the cement
detonated red bombs.

Now I am grownup
and literate, and I sit in my chair
as quietly as a fuse

and the jungles are flaming, the under-
brush is charged with soldiers,
the names on the difficult
maps go up in smoke.

I am the cause, I am a stockpile of chemical
toys, my body
is a deadly gadget,
I reach out in love, my hands are guns,
my good intentions are completely lethal.

Even my
passive eyes transmute
everything I look at to the pocked
black and white of a war photo,
how
can I stop myself

3 ⚭ *Transformational Voices Enter the Conversation*

In recent years a third set of understandings has emerged describing what preaching is all about. This new set of understandings is not a single, well-articulated theory but a variety of claims that share common convictions, emphases, and presuppositions. Or, imaged differently, this third understanding of preaching is a large umbrella under which stand a number of homiletical scholars. While their views of preaching are not reducible to a unified theory, they do evidence certain similarities that represent extensions of and shifts away from traditional and kerygmatic understandings of preaching.

Paul S. Wilson identifies "new directions" in preaching and writes of "an apparent convergence of thought in the work of some of the people who have helped shape the new directions, people such as Elizabeth Achtemeier, Charles Bartow, Frederick Buechner, David Buttrick, Fred B. Craddock, H. Grady Davis, Eugene L. Lowry, Morris J. Niedenthal, Charles L. Rice, Edmund Steimle, Thomas H. Troeger, Robert Waznak, and others" (1988, 22–23). While my umbrella is probably larger than Wilson's, I also recognize a "convergence of thought" (ibid.) among a number of homiletical scholars who are redescribing preaching's purpose, content, language, and form.

If traditional, kerygmatic, and transformational understandings of preaching were arranged along a continuum, on one end would be traditional homiletical theory. Partially overlapping with traditional theory and adding its own distinctive convictions and emphases is kerygmatic theory. Partially overlapping with kerygmatic theory and breaking new ground is the umbrella I am calling "transformational understandings of preaching." This image of the continuum, however, is only partially accurate because some transformational views of preaching share a few convictions in common with traditional theory that are not present in kerygmatic theory.

Listening

"Transformational" is only one label for these recent understandings of preaching. Others, reflecting different emphases, are "word-event," "existential," "poetic," "narrative," "imaginative," and "creative." I have chosen the term "transformational" because it conveys the commonly held belief that a sermon should be an experience that transforms the worshipers.

Purpose

An important conviction of transformational preaching is reflected in the following critical comment on a sermon: "It wrestled tolerably well with the *idea* of transparency but conveyed the *experience* of transparency less ably" (Sider and King 1987, 16). According to transformational understandings of preaching, whatever else a sermon does, its primary purpose is to facilitate an experience, an event, a meeting, or a happening for the worshipers. Paul Scherer claims, "Something has to happen—there is no other goal for preaching: a meeting has to take place; the sermon has no other aim" (1965, 72). Scherer's views are close to kerygmatic theory in that the goal of every sermon is a meeting or encounter with Christ. The views of Bruce C. Salmon move away from kerygmatic theory: A particular sermon might aim to help the congregation not only "hear about forgiveness" but also "feel forgiven" (1988, 96).

Transformational understandings of preaching share with kerygmatic theory this emphasis on preaching's goal as an event. Missing or de-emphasized is kerygmatic theory's claim that preaching's goal is also the communication of the *kerygma,* the gospel, or the Word as fixed content. Scherer, for example, minimizing a sermon's cognitive content, claims that God does not "send me a message" (1965, 48). Rather, "God's good news . . . is concerned with response to a Person" (51); it is about a relationship with Christ, "about nothing more, and about nothing less" (53). This almost exclusive focus on preaching's "eventfulness" (Randolph 1969, 1), divorced from the transmission of fixed content, is new in descriptions of preaching's purpose under the transformational umbrella.

A second shift in emphasis is also new. Kerygmatic theory emphasizes God's responsibility in the sermon's becoming an event. The preacher's task is simply to preach the *kerygma;* if the *kerygma* is truly preached, an encounter with God occurs. Transformational preaching emphasizes more the preacher's responsibility in the sermon's becoming an event. This emphasis on the preacher's responsibility is especially evident in discussions of such hows of preaching as language and form.

Transformational views of preaching's purpose differ from kerygmatic views finally because of a third shift in emphasis. In kerygmatic theory, the dominant focus is on the divine side of the divine-human encounter. The sermon's goal is an event that mediates God and knowledge of God through divine self-revelation. In transformational views of preaching, the dominant focus shifts to the human side of the encounter. Preaching's goal is to facilitate a sermonic event that changes the worshiper's values, worldviews, or reality. Preaching's goal is "a transformation so deep that it changes [the worshiper's] whole life" (Grasso 1965, 145). Charles L. Rice echoes kerygmatic language: preaching's aim is "a meeting, . . . an encounter with God" (1970, 15). His description of the result of that encounter shifts him under the transformational umbrella: A sermon should be an event that "*effects* a new kind of seeing" (45) or a "new understanding of oneself and one's tradition" (21). Similarly, Charles L. Bartow echoes kerygmatic theory: "Preaching is not just the proclamation of an event—even of The Event; it *is* an event—a happening, an experience" (1980, 18). And the result of the preaching event? The transformation of "what is" in the direction of "what yet may be" (18). According to Bartow, the preaching event discloses "new ways . . . of being and acting in the world" (20).

These transformational understandings of preaching's purpose involve new roles for the preacher and the congregation. The preacher comes down off a pedestal and stands under the Word along with the congregation. And the members of the congregation are invited to participate more substantially in the sermonic event.

Fred B. Craddock (1974) discusses the changed role of the preacher. The preacher should above all be "a listener to the Word of God" (43), seeking to experience the Word as "an event" or "a happening" (35). In addition, the preacher should "really be a member of the congregation" (83), able "to be vulnerable" (82) and to live and preach in "relationship with the people" (83). Preachers who are open to God's active Word and to the lives of the congregation do not expect the congregation to "tune in on [their] broadcast" (43).

New roles also emerge for the members of the congregation. Craddock's caricature of their earlier role is that of javelin catcher (55). In his alternative proposal, preaching engages the congregation in active participation both while the sermon is being preached and after its conclusion. While the sermon is being preached, it should activate meanings in the lives of the members of the congregation and enable them to reflect on their lives in the light of the gospel. It should encourage the members of the congregation to fill in the sermonic details (93) and arrive at their own conclusions (62). And after the sermon has ended, the members of the congregation should find themselves "thinking their own thoughts, dealing with their own situations, and being responsible for their own faith" (157). Craddock warns that a sermon that appears to invite the congregation to draw their own conclusions and in reality limits their response to a single choice is deceptive (67). For Craddock, the primary goal of preaching is "transformation" (21), or "a recreation of the way life is experienced" (80). His claim is that transformation happens when the people reflect on their lives in a new way, "a way that is provided by the Gospel" (73). The active participation of the people leads not to their acceptance or rejection of the message, as in traditional and kerygmatic theories, but to their own particular conclusions that are capable of transforming their particular lives.

Directly attacking "the distance between speaker and hearer" (19), Craddock characterizes the new relationship with the words "democracy," "dialogue," and "listening by the speaker" coupled with "contributing by the hearer" (55). Paul S. Wilson similarly describes this new relationship: "As preachers, we do not stand against the people, untouched by their temptations or struggles. We stand *with* the people, as one of them, under the Word" (1988, 29). Standing thus under the Word, the preacher first and then the congregation through the sermon experience the Word as a transforming event.

Content

These understandings of preaching's purpose are intricately bound up with understandings of preaching's content. If preaching's content in traditional theory is universal or propositional truth and its content in kerygmatic theory is kerygmatic truth, its content under the transformational umbrella is not as easy to identify. Perhaps "existential truth," broadly defined, both hints at the commonly held convictions and emphases and reflects shared understandings of the Word, the *kerygma,* revelation, and truth. Undergirding all these new convictions and emphases is a general shift in emphasis from epistemology to hermeneutics.

"Existential truth" explicitly identifies the content of preaching for some scholars under the transformational umbrella. Craddock writes that "the subject matter [of preaching] is not the nature of God but the hearer's situation in the light of God" (1974, 59). Other scholars link preaching with a new way of "perceiving reality" (Salmon 1988, 97; see also Claypool 1980, 78), "truth—about ourselves and the world" (Rice 1970, 45), and "a fresh worldview, . . . a fresh self-view, a fresh God-view" (Halvorson 1982, 69). The influences of Greek Testament scholar Rudolf Bultmann and theologian Paul Tillich are evident in these descriptions of preaching's content as new self-understanding, new insight into human existence, or existential truth.

A recurring theme in this version of transformational preaching is that preaching replaces one set of understandings with another. For Milton Crum, Jr., preaching substitutes the "verbal map of the biblical faith" for the wisdom of the world (1977, 36). For Arndt L. Halvorson, preaching provides "a totally new *belief system*" (1982, 47). For both Craddock and Elizabeth R. Achtemeier, preaching exchanges one set of images for another (Craddock 1974, 78–79; Achtemeier 1980, 24). These scholars describe preaching's content as, at least in part, a new way of perceiving or being in the world.

Other scholars under the transformational umbrella echo kerygmatic theory so that the existential character of preaching's content is less obvious. Scherer, for example, insists that preaching is not about a worldview or a way of life (1965, 50, 52) but about the gospel, which is "the dramatic encounter between God in Christ and the human soul" (49). The content of preaching is solely the gospel. Yet Scherer identifies the gospel as being like a phone call: "On the instant the whole situation was transformed. A higher order of reality had cut across my existence" (49). Scherer also likens the gospel to an announcement that one's "house is on fire" (19) or that "the new age has come, the new creation" (48). Thus, though preaching's content for Scherer is the gospel, he equates the gospel with a new reality that results in the transformation of "the stuff of human existence" (19).

Domenico Grasso echoes both traditional and kerygmatic theory while standing under the transformational umbrella (1965). In line with traditional theory, he identifies preaching's content as a message that must be transmitted (243). In line with kerygmatic theory, he equates this message with "Christ" (20). In answer to the question "What is being preached?" (1), Grasso answers "Christ" (6, 21). Grasso's elaboration of this message shifts him under the transformational umbrella and manifests the existential dimension of preaching's content. A message, according to Grasso, is "a revolt against reality, an attempt to transform it, to change the course of things" (19). Christ, as preaching's message, totally transforms life, producing a "new orientation" and new values (151). Preaching Christ "radically alters [a person's] situation on earth" (58).

These convictions about the what of preaching presuppose new understandings of the Word of God, the *kerygma,* revelation, and truth.

As in kerygmatic theory, the catalyst for the sermonic event is the active Word of God. Transformational preaching, however, emphasizes how the Word affects human existence. Bartow, for example, shares with kerygmatic theory a conviction that the Word possesses "dynamic, creative power" (1980, 49). At the same time, he is only minimally concerned with its ability to disclose the nature of God, an essential function of the Word in kerygmatic theory. His focus is the Word's "power to bring into one's purview what was not there before; the power to select and arrange, to order and locate people and things—the cosmos itself!" (49). Under the transformational umbrella the Word is directed toward "people and things—the cosmos itself" (ibid.).

In kerygmatic theory, the Word is primary as the bringer of truth; the world or human existence is secondary, important only because there truth is applied. In transformational views of preaching, the Word and the world are inseparable. The Word interprets and changes human existence; the world is that arena where the Word is active.

A consequence of this new understanding of the Word of God is that the Word is no longer restricted primarily to the Bible, as in kerygmatic theory. Rice claims the Word "happens" not just in the reading of Scripture and the delivery of a sermon, but also in the world, in human nature, and, especially, in art (1970, 6, 41, 83, 109). It "breaks out in cultural forms" (6). In particular, in the preacher's humanity, the Word once again becomes flesh (78). This understanding of the Word of God shares with traditional homiletics the claim that the Word is operative in creation, history, nature, as well as in the Bible and preaching.

Finally, some transformational views of the Word differ from kerygmatic views in that the objectivity of the Word is no longer stressed. Craddock argues that to conceive of the Word as though it could be "spoken into an empty room or into the wind . . . is a contradiction of what a word is" (1974, 70). The Word, he continues, "is a call, and a call is meaningless without a hearer" (70). For Craddock, the Word "has its existence" only in "listening-speaking-listening," only "in the sharing" (71).

Changes in meaning also accompany the *kerygma,* a term infrequently used by transformational scholars. When the word appears, it never designates a fixed formula of essential tenets. Instead, it refers to a narrative of events: for example, Jesus' life, death, and resurrection (Bartow 1980, 19) or "a summary of the history of salvation, the story of the divine plan of God's encounter with [humanity]" (Grasso 1964, 233). A redefined *kerygma* underlies Grasso's claim about preaching that takes the *kerygma* as its norm, a claim that sets it apart from both traditional and kerygmatic theories: such preaching "should seek to enlarge upon a series of events rather than to draw out ideas or build up a system of dogma and morality" (234).

Similarly, new meanings also accompany the term *revelation.* Echoing kerygmatic homiletical theory, Grasso describes revelation as both an event and doctrine (1965, 17). Yet his emphasis is on revelation's historical dimension as "God's intervention in space and time" (33; see also 250). Grasso de-emphasizes revelation's doctrinal dimension, or "the intellectual angle of truth manifested by God" (32–33). Scherer likewise echoes kerygmatic theory and describes revelation as an event that "has to do with the imparting of oneself" (1965, 31). Yet for Scherer, revelation's content can never be known with certainty (28). Revelation becomes a "ceaseless activity" that "lays hold on everything and appropriates what it will. It leaves nothing unchanged. It fashions and transforms" (21). As with the *kerygma,* revelation as fixed content is de-emphasized or missing altogether. Revelation has become an event in history that transforms human existence.

These shifts in the meanings of the Word, the *kerygma,* and revelation are linked to similar shifts in the meaning of the word *truth.* For some scholars under the transformational umbrella, truth remains objective and "timeless," although what is important is that it "must be heard as timely" (Halvorson 1982, 69), able to "break through to our awareness" (84).

Other transformational scholars define truth differently. H. Grady Davis writes, "the truth we preach is not an abstract thing. The truth is a Person" (1958, 19). He continues:

> The goodness we preach is not an ideal quality. The goodness is Someone who is good. The truth, the goodness we preach is not a thing that can first be defined and then applied to God, to Christ. The truth, the goodness, is God in Christ. (19)

This truth is known in a "living existential person-to-person relationship" (v).

For Davis and some other transformational scholars, truth characterizes the divine-human relationship. For other transformational scholars, truth shifts to the realm of human existence. Frederick Buechner describes truth as "what is, the good with the bad, the joy with the despair, the presence and absence of God, the swollen eye, the bird pecking the cobbles for crumbs" (1977, 16).

Such shifts surrounding the word *truth* necessitate new understandings of what the preacher gleans from the Bible. Traditional and kerygmatic theories sent preachers to the Bible in search of universal or gospel truths. Achtemeier, however, challenges such scriptural treasure hunts and claims that "the Bible's message cannot be reduced to 'timeless truths'" (1980, 55). Instead "the message of a single text may be entirely different from year to year, as the situation of the people changes, and this is why we never can claim we know what the Bible says. We may know what it said last month, but what does it say this month?" (55).

New understandings of the Word, the *kerygma,* revelation, and truth participate in a general shift that characterizes many scholars under the transformational umbrella and distances them from both traditional and kerygmatic scholars. This is a shift from epistemology to hermeneutics. Many scholars under the transformational umbrella reflect a diminishing confidence in epistemological methods for discerning objective truth. They no longer seek to ground preaching in theology in general or in biblical theology, which particularly supports kerygmatic theory. Instead, the focus shifts to the interpretation of texts or, more specifically, to the power that texts have for shaping meaning in the interpreter.

A significant theme in transformational views of preaching is an eroding confidence that theology can provide preaching's content. Traditional and kerygmatic theories assume that theology can and should state the content of the Word and revelation. Theology thus provides the norms by which preaching's content is reckoned as truth.[1] But for many under the transformational umbrella, theology ceases to constitute a single system capable of producing truth. Thor Hall describes two approaches to theology (1971). The first is theology as a unified system that defines truth as absolute and transcendent (48). For some theologians who use this approach, discerning truth requires the aid of human reason. For others, truth is revealed and stands opposed to every human effort. In both instances, these theologians assume a single way to know absolute truth (48). This first approach to theology undergirds both traditional theory, which values human reason in the process of arriving at truth, and kerygmatic theory, which defines truth as revealed. Hall then identifies a second, emergent approach to theology, which posits truth as "a larger, pluralistic, many-faceted truth complex" (48–49). This second approach to theology, coupled with eight theological methodologies that Hall describes (51–54), undermines the image of theology as a single system that can provide the unambiguous, normative content for preaching.

Hall's second image of truth as pluralistic and many-faceted is echoed by a number of homiletical scholars under the transformational umbrella. For these

scholars, God's Word, revelation, and sermonic truth are fleeting and fragmented. Robert D. Young claims, "We live . . . by every word that proceeds from
the mouth of God—which we receive in momentary outcroppings of insight"
(1979, 171). John Killinger writes of "pieces of revelation" (1969, 23). Thomas H.
Troeger images the preacher's words as "particles of truth" (1982, 19).

When theology no longer constitutes a single system, the task of identifying preaching's content is complicated. Robert W. Duke describes five contemporary theologies (1980): neoorthodoxy, existentialism, liberalism, funda-
mentalism, and Black liberationism. He concludes, "We all preach the crucified
Christ, but the meaning of that proclamation is the subject of considerable difference of interpretation" (97).

Few scholars under the transformational umbrella expressly acknowledge
William J. Hill's claim that "theological pluralism is a *fait accompli*" (1983, 124).
Yet many reflect a waning confidence in theology and its ability to formulate
statements of changeless truth that then constitute preaching's content.

This waning confidence also affects biblical theology that particularly
grounds preaching's content in kerygmatic theory. Biblical theology is the do-
main of those biblical scholars who claim, through using categories of thought
arising out of texts, to discover the Bible's essential teachings. From biblical theology arises kerygmatic theory's belief that the sermon's content, the gospel's
core or the *kerygma,* has been faithfully extracted from the Bible. For many under the transformational umbrella, biblical theology is equally unable to produce preaching's normative content as the *kerygma* or core biblical truths.

Thomas H. Keir describes his disappointment with biblical scholarship
(1962). He does not question that biblical scholars should both interpret what
passages of Scripture mean (71, 90) and provide preachers with the proper interpretive method (68). His claim, however, is that they have failed. In the face
of their failure he asks, "What then is the preacher to do so long as the debate
of the [biblical] scholars is inconclusive?" He continues: "The answer surely is
plain. [Preachers] must enter into the Bible's imagination and [they] must use
[their] own" (69). Preachers thus become interpreters, trying to discern the intention of the biblical writers (69–70). Yet their study of Scripture will produce
no final, fixed interpretations. Keir invites preachers to wrestle with biblical
texts and images, without a promise of final certitude about their meaning for
the first century or for the twentieth (see 74, 76, 90). Keir finally leaves preachers struggling to interpret biblical interpretations of mystery (71, 77).

Although many scholars who advocate transformational views of preaching
are more confident than Keir about the results of interpretation, Keir reflects the
shift from epistemology to hermeneutics, from certain theological knowledge
extracted from the Bible to the interpretation of meaning in particular biblical
texts. Transformational scholars tend to link preaching's content with texts and
their ongoing interpretation. This shift to hermeneutics coincides with new convictions about the nature and function of language to which we now turn.

Language

What is particularly distinctive about transformational understandings of preaching are new assumptions about language. The sermon's words continue to be the locus for an encounter or an event. But discussions of language under the transformational umbrella tend not to focus on the unchanging reality behind the words, as in traditional and kerygmatic theories. The focus instead is on the change in the human situation created by the words.

Four convictions are distinctive. First, language shapes human consciousness and therefore has the power to bring about changes in perception, values, or worldviews. Second, words both say things and do things; or, stated differently, words are events. This conviction reflects the influences of speech act theory and the new hermeneutic. The third conviction is the belief in the importance of poetic language. On the one hand, this emphasis on poetic language corresponds to a new focus on the mystery of God that demands language that is imaginative, evocative, even ambiguous. This emphasis on the mystery of God tends to replace kerygmatic theory's emphasis on knowledge about God. On the other hand, poetic language is also important because of its ability to change human consciousness. Fourth, the relationship between language, particularly sermonic language, and human experience is important. Each of these deserves attention.

1. Words shape human consciousness. This is a primary conviction about language in most transformational understandings of preaching. Language reflects a construct of reality in human consciousness and organizes a person's perception of the world. Following Martin Heidegger, Craddock claims that "reality is linguistically constructed, for language is the 'house of being'" (1974, 36). Our "very being . . . is founded in language" (37). Similarly, Achtemeier claims that "language brings reality into being for a person and orders and shapes the person's universe" (1980, 23). For her, "if we want to change someone's life . . . , we must change the images—the imaginations of the heart—in short, the words by which that person lives" (24). To change language is to change the inner construct of reality. New language brings new reality into being. Two significant emphases here are the correspondence between words and a construct in human consciousness and the power of words to create new constructs.[2]

2. Words are events. A second conviction about language that characterizes transformational views of preaching is that words both say things and do things, that words are events. Two influences here are speech act theory and the new hermeneutic.

Speech act theory is not a single theory but subsumes a number of positions that continue the work of J. L. Austin, an English philosopher of language (White 1988, 1–4). Austin distinguishes between a "constative" statement that describes or reports a truth or falsehood (Austin 1975, 3) and a "performative" statement that performs an action (6). Examples of performative utterances

include "I do," "I give and bequeath . . . ," "I bet you" (5), and "I promise
to . . ." (9). In a performative utterance, one is "not, or not merely, saying something but doing something" (25). The distinction here is between different
types of statements—those that "say" something only and those that both "say"
and "do" something. Austin finally, however, shifts his focus from these two
types of statements to a more general "theory of speech-acts" (148, 150). His
new concern becomes the "illocutionary force" of all utterances (109–32), that
is, what "we are performing" in speaking (150).

Craddock is a primary channel through which Austin's insights entered
homiletical theory (1974). Craddock claims, "Words not only report something;
they do something" (34). He laments that too often today words simply describe: they "serve only as signs pointing to the discovered or discoverable
data" (33). But, Craddock continues, "before they were smothered by a scientific and technological culture," words "danced, sang, teased, lured, probed,
wept, judged, and transformed" (34). Craddock's conviction is that a word is
"an action, something happening" (44): "words are deeds" (34). And his hope
is to recover the "dynamistic and creative functions of language" (34).

Other scholars under the transformational umbrella echo speech act theory
in their description of the link between biblical interpretation and preaching.
For example, Sheldon A. Tostengard proposes that a sermon should seek "to
'do' the text for the hearer" (1989, 78).

Also undergirding transformational preaching's conviction that words are
events is the new hermeneutic.[3] Formulated by Ernst Fuchs and Gerhard Ebeling among others, the new hermeneutic is a theory of language, a method of
reading biblical texts, and a theology of the Word of God and proclamation.
Underlying the new hermeneutic is the conviction that words happen (Ebeling 1963, 319). Therefore, texts, which consist of words, are "word-events"
(319). To be understood, texts must once again become events; that is, they
must generate in the interpreter new self-understanding or new insight into reality. Interpretation demands from the interpreter both participation and existential decision. Only after interpreters have been interpreted by the text can
they become preachers. Ebeling argues that "a sermon is not exposition of the
text as past proclamation, but is itself proclamation in the present—and that
means, then, that *the sermon is* EXECUTION *of the text*" (331). In other words,
the preacher's task is to recreate in the sermon the word-event present in the
text so that the sermon becomes a similar word-event for the congregation.

The claim that language is eventful is of critical importance to scholars under the transformational umbrella both in the interpreting of texts and in the
shaping of sermons. For Thomas G. Long, the preacher, while studying a text,
is "expecting something to happen, expecting some eventful word that makes
a critical difference for the life of the church" (1989b, 84). Then as the preacher
begins to shape the sermon, "what the biblical text intends to say and do now
becomes what the preacher hopes to say and do in the sermon" (86).

This conviction that language is eventful undergirds the shift from epistemology to hermeneutics. Traditional and kerygmatic scholars whose concern is epistemology approach a text expecting to discover an unchanging truth that they can extract and formulate into their sermon's focal idea. Transformational scholars whose concern is hermeneutics approach a text "listening for a voice, looking for a presence, hoping for the claim of God to be encountered through the text" (ibid., 44). Undergirding such listening, looking, and hoping is the presupposition that the text is "a living language voice in search of a hearer, a voice which seeks to break in upon us from beyond" (Tostengard 1989, 81).

   3. Poetic language. A third conviction characteristic of many discussions of transformational preaching is the importance of poetic or metaphoric language. If the goal of preaching is first and foremost an encounter or event, Keir asks a critical question, "What is the language of primary encounter?" (1962, 63; see Sittler 1966, 19). His answer is poetic language—"images, analogies, parables, metaphors, paradigms" (65). Keir distinguishes between abstract language (64) and poetic language, which he calls "the language of the human heart, of 'the lover and the sage'" (91).

   Other homiletical scholars make similar distinctions. Rice describes the positivist's contrast between scientific or referential language, which allows one to "speak sensibly," and emotive language, which leads one "to spout nonsense" (1970, 37). The positivist values the former as "the only real language" (39). Rice reverses the hierarchy and values the latter, which he redefines as the language of the poet that is "indispensable to the human spirit" (39). Don M. Wardlaw, following literary critic Philip Wheelwright, distinguishes between "static language," which seeks "to eliminate ambiguity," and "tensive language," which "risks ambiguity on the wings of metaphor, image, parable, fable, and simile" (1983, 19). Wardlaw prefers tensive language because of its power "to create new possibilities for the reader or hearer to see What Is" (19).

   Keir's reasons for preferring images or poetic language are worth summarizing because they undergird many discussions of transformational preaching. First, Keir claims that poetic images link the Unseen with the seen. He believes that a critical problem for the "Western world" is the "numbing of the sense of the Unseen," a problem that in part has "to do with language and forms of thought" (1962, 90). The task before every preacher is to recover "a feeling for poetry" (67) because poetic language is the medium by which the worshipers become "aware of the Unseen, or, even more explicitly, they encounter God" (62).

   For Keir, images are important for a second reason. Not only are they the locus for encounters with the Unseen, but they are all that is available of the Unseen. Quoting Austin Farrer, Keir claims that "we cannot point away from the revealed images to an imageless or 'straight' truth which the images signify," or, again, "we cannot bypass the images to seize an imageless truth."[4] Emphasizing the inescapable nature of the image, Keir again quotes Farrer, "It is only in being aware of something finite as an analogy of God that we begin to be aware of God at all."[5] Images are indispensable as the "technicalities" from which the preacher cannot escape (77–78).

Images are important for a third reason, because they link the Unseen with the seen, with the emphasis this time on the world that is seen. The preacher must interpret the biblical image in light of "the everyday image" (83) so that the congregation can begin to recognize and name daily experiences with the Unseen (82). The preacher must interpret "everyday things" so that they may "be viewed with a refreshed sense of wonder" (83).

Other scholars under the transformational umbrella place greater emphasis than Keir on the ability of poetic language to transform the seen or what is. Charles L. Bartow claims that religious or metaphorical language "is aimed at *evoking* reality" (1980, 18). He explains that a sermon refers or points neither to "something in the past" nor to "any individual, thing, or circumstance of the present"; "instead, the referent of a sermon is what lies beyond. Preaching has to do with what yet may be" (18). This "what yet may be" consists of "new possibilities" (19) for "being and acting in the world" (20). Poetic language is essential because it evokes, creates, or brings into being God's new reality for human life. Poetic language is eventful language by which we encounter the divine and by which we find our perceptions and ways of being in the world transformed.

4. The relationship between language and experience. This discussion of poetic language leads to a fourth conviction characteristic of many transformational views of preaching—that the relationship between language and human experience is crucially important. Scholars under the transformational umbrella generally agree that sermonic language should reflect human experience, because human existence is the object of transformation. These same scholars, however, diverge widely in their specific discussions of the issue.

Wardlaw places emphasis on the preacher's "personal journey into the hidden depths" (1983, 19), a journey that enables the preacher to choose sermonic language that is "tensive." "Tensive language" invites the congregation to enter the journey of the preacher and "to experience reality in personal and suggestive ways" (19).

Craddock places emphasis on the ordinary experiences of life that are apparent when the preacher's imagination "walks down the streets where we live" (1974, 80). The preacher's imagination should reflect the congregation's world so that sermons become "real" (80).

More radically, William L. Malcomson suggests replacing the language of inherited theology with the language of ordinary experience (1968). He describes a "T group" in which "instead of using the word 'salvation,' we spoke of getting to know people more deeply and getting to understand ourselves more fully. Instead of 'redemption,' we spoke of caring about other people, really being concerned. Instead of 'sin,' we spoke of self-hate, hurting the other person, treating another person as a thing" (126–27). Because Malcomson's

concern is not religious truths but simply "truths" (127) or "what is really going on" (107), he insists that all sermonic language should be ordinary, non-
theological language.

For Rice, the issue is not intentionally replacing one set of words with another but recognizing the inevitable subjective link between all language and
human experience (1970). The issue is not that sermonic language *ought* to reflect human experience but that it *inevitably* reflects human experience. Rice's
claim is that all "talk about God" is grounded in human subjectivity (13). For
Rice, theology as it "appears in Christian preaching" is "the distinctive shape
which the preacher gives to experience" (91). Likewise, both exegesis and application are "existential" in that they are "filtered through the preacher's own
subjective awareness" (95). For Rice, all language reflects the user's experience.

Among these transformational scholars, the common thread is the importance of the linkage between language, particularly sermonic language, and
life.

These new convictions about the nature and function of both language in
general and sermonic language in particular distinguish transformational views
of preaching from traditional and kerygmatic views. If language is inseparable
from paradigms in human consciousness and if language changes result in paradigm changes, then words are at the heart of preaching's ability to transform
human existence. For some transformational scholars, shaping the sermon as a
word-event requires that the preacher be sensitive to both poetic language and
the language of human experience. In addition, for some transformational scholars, shaping the sermon as a word-event also requires attention to how the sermon's words are put together. The result is an emphasis on sermonic form.

Form

Scherer uses standard labels to describe the forms of the sermons in which
he puts into practice his suggestions about homiletical theory (1965). His sermons, he says, are "expository and doctrinal" (xii). Here Scherer is representative of those scholars for whom transformational convictions about preaching are divorced from innovative thinking about sermonic forms.

For many transformational scholars, however, rethinking preaching's purpose, content, and language entails rethinking preaching's forms. These scholars seem to be asking a reformulation of Keir's question "What is the language
of primary encounter?" (1962, 63). The reformulated question is, What is the
form of primary encounter or of preaching as a transforming event?

The scholars who discuss innovative forms of the sermon tend to agree that
the sermon's form should replicate or convey a prior experience. They dis-
agree, however, as to the nature of that prior experience. On the one hand are
those scholars for whom the sermon's form should be controlled exclusively
by the biblical text. On the other hand are those for whom the sermon's form
should reflect the preacher's personal experience of wrestling with a text.

By and large, the emphasis falls on the intention of the original biblical author or the intention encoded in the language of the text. Halvorson calls the sermon "a reenactment of the original message" or "the refleshing of the message" (1982, 47). Ronald J. Allen contends that "the purpose of preaching on a parable is to re-create with the congregation the experience embodied in the parable" (1983, 40). Other scholars write of "replicating . . . [the] text's performative purpose in the mind of the hearers" (Eslinger 1987, 143) and of regenerating the text's claim (Long 1989a, 33).

David James Randolph discusses an approach to sermonic form that links the text as an event with the sermon as an event (1969). According to Randolph, a sermon should carry "forward the intentionality of the biblical text by following the arc of action called for by the biblical word to its point of intersection with the contemporary congregation" (30). New forms are needed because neither of the two standard sermonic forms is capable of accomplishing this task. By the two standard forms, Randolph means "the statement of propositions derived from the text" (103), a form characteristic of traditional homiletics, and "the verse-by-verse exposition of a scriptural passage" (103), a form advocated by some kerygmatic homiletical scholars. Randolph proposes an alternative approach to sermonic form in which the sermon becomes an "adventure" (105). His alternative approach takes account of both "the literary shape of the text" and "the intention and mood of the text" (106).

Randolph discusses four biblical forms suggestive of homiletical forms. One is poetry, with its rhythms and imagery. Preaching that is poetic "does not so much state a thesis as create an effect" (107). A second is story, which invites the congregation to participate in the narrative movement (111). Two other biblical forms are the essay or personal reflection (115–18) and oratory (119–23). Whatever the form, Randolph claims that one mark of good sermon structure is progressive movement: "The sermon should capture our attention at the beginning and take us on an ascending line toward the climax" (127). Thus, "every sermon is a safari" (127).

Randolph recognizes that these forms serve a different purpose from earlier forms and therefore require a new understanding of how such sermons should be evaluated. The new forms facilitate an event. Therefore any evaluation of such a sermon should focus on the question "What *happened* in this sermon?" (132). Such an evaluation "is person-centered rather than proposition-centered" (132).

Expanding Randolph's forms, Allen suggests how the preacher might shape sermons in the form of "wisdom sayings, the various types of commandments, beatitudes, catalogs of virtues and vices" (1983, 37). He invites the preacher to rediscover the experience that gave rise to the text and to create a similar experience for the contemporary congregation (37–38).

Long takes up Randolph's discussion of shaping the sermon at the intersection of the text's intentionality and the contemporary congregation (1989a,

1989b). Long proposes that a "text possesses its own unique and complex set of intentionalities" (1989b, 84). Preachers should pay attention to the effects that a text intends to have on its reader by assessing its literary genre—whether it is a psalm, proverb, narrative, parable, or epistle—and the corresponding rhetorical devices. The preacher can then shape a sermon that will "create a similar effect for hearers" (1989a, 50).

For some scholars under the transformational umbrella, the focus is exclusively on the biblical text. Because the sermon should recreate for the congregation an experience of the intention of the text or a contemporary counterpart of that intention, the text's form holds clues for the sermon's form.

Other scholars emphasize the preacher's personal experience of the text. Troeger reflects this shift in emphasis when he asks:

What does the passage make me want to do?

> Clap my hands and sing?
> Get on my knees and pray?
> Write my congressional representative?

And how is God reshaping me through the text?

> By speaking through a metaphor that sends a rush of hope to my heart?
> By telling a story that shines a searchlight on my life?
> By touching my wounds and filling me with strength? (1983, 154)

For Craddock, the sermon should aim to recreate the preacher's experience, "to reflect it, not simply reflect upon it" (1974, 77). While both of these scholars continue to stress the importance of the biblical text, the focus shifts to the preacher's experience of the text.

The preacher's first task is to experience the Word. The second is to recreate for the congregation what the preacher has experienced (see Rice 1983, 104).

Recreating the preacher's wrestling with texts demands innovative sermon forms. Three scholars who contribute to this discussion are Davis, Craddock, and Lowry. Among their legacies are three particular forms: the story-sermon, the inductive sermon, and the narrative sermon.

Davis, to a large extent, set the stage for recent innovations in sermonic form (1958). One of his primary legacies is his image of sermon making as an organic process in which a "generative idea" produces the sermon's form (21). What one says in a sermon, the sermon's content or substance, and how one says it, the sermon's form, are not two separate processes. Unlike traditional and kerygmatic preachers, Davis's preacher does not first discern the sermon's message and then find a form to communicate it. Instead, form grows organically out of the changes the generative idea produces in the preacher.

And what is the generative idea? It is an insight that is "productive," "germinal" (21, 58), or "fruitful" (58) within the life of the preacher. It is an idea that is able "to pierce the preacher first of all" (58; see also 43). In discussing his generative idea, Davis focuses not on the text's intention but on the preacher's experience.

And how does the generative idea produce a sermon? Once it "comes alive in the preacher [it] has power to expand into a living sermon" (82) by producing "an experience shared by preacher and people" (188).

Davis's legacy also includes his image of the sermon as "an audible movement in time" (22). The sermon is to generate an experience for the congregation (170); therefore the sermon's continuity or movement presents "a problem which must be solved for the listener, from [the listener's] point of view, not from the point of view of the preacher" (164). Davis discusses five types of sermonic movement or continuity. Two of these types bore fruit in the work of Craddock, whose inductive method is similar to Davis's inductive continuity (175–77), and Lowry, whose narrative method is similar to Davis's chronological and narrative continuity (180–84).

Davis's legacy also includes the particular sermonic structure, "a story told" (157–62). In describing this form, he offers insights that are similar to and different from discussions of story preaching by traditional and kerygmatic scholars. Like them, Davis never discards the conviction that the sermon grows from a generative idea. The sermon as "a story told" should be built around an "idea" (157), "principle theme" (159), "important message" (161), or "point" (161). At the same time, Davis's hope is that in story preaching a worshiper identifies "with the characters . . . , lives through the incidents with them, understands their motives, and renders [a personal] verdict on their opinions, character, and actions" (161). For Davis, the worshipers have a degree of freedom to interpret the story-sermon for themselves. Unlike traditional and kerygmatic scholars who insist that the worshipers arrive at the preacher's conclusion, Davis wants the worshipers to "draw [their] own conclusions and make [their] own application to" their lives (161). Davis warns those preachers who "cannot trust [their] hearers to do this, . . . not [to] use the story form" (161). Overinterpreting destroys "the inherent force of the narrative" (161). Undergirding the sermon as "a story told" is Davis's belief in "the power of a narrative to communicate meaning and influence the lives of our people" (158).

Davis's interest is restricted to biblical narratives. He insists he is not encouraging preachers to "construct fictional narratives or fictionalize the narratives in the Gospels" (158). Those who came after him, however, embraced both fictional stories and fictionalized biblical stories as legitimate forms of story preaching. What the sermon as story gives to transformational preaching is a form that crafts an experience for the congregation that is based on the preacher's prior experience.

A second scholar whose innovative work on sermonic form is significant in transformational preaching and who highlights the preacher's experience of the text is Craddock (1974). What is the form of the sermon as transforming event? Craddock believes it is the inductive sermon. On the one hand, Craddock links the inductive form to the message of the text (125) or "*the point* the author sought to make" (105). The sermon should be "proclamation of that which the text proclaimed" (123). On the other hand, he also links the inductive form to the preacher's experience of the text. Where does an inductive sermon begin? Craddock writes that "anyone who has been thrilled, frightened, moved, paralyzed, honored, humbled, and inescapably addressed by [Jesus'] simple call, 'Follow me,' has the basic raw material for a sermon" (140).

How is an inductive sermon shaped? It recreates for the congregation the preacher's experience of arriving at the text's message. It retraces the preacher's experience of "conceiving an idea, playing with it, wrestling with it, and bringing it to clarity" (162). By capturing in words "the sights and sounds of [the preacher's] experience," the inductive sermon hopes "the congregation can hear what [the preacher] has heard" (77). Craddock's hope is that both the preacher and the congregation will arrive at the same conclusion (57, 162). He nevertheless insists that the congregation must be given the freedom to complete the sermon's "thought, movement and decision-making" (64; see also 146). The inductive form thus becomes a vehicle by which preachers shape an experience for the congregation out of their own experience of arriving at a text's meaning.

Another scholar whose sermon design reflects the preacher's experience of wrestling with a text is Lowry (1980, 1985, 1989, 1990). Lowry provides another answer to the question, What is the form of the sermon as transforming event? He offers the narrative sermon. For Lowry, the narrative sermon is distinct from the story-sermon (1989, 14). The "story-sermon" is a sermon that tells a story. The "narrative sermon" is a sermon that follows the sequential elements of a plot.

Lowry's definition of a plot varies. In *Doing Time in the Pulpit* (1985) he describes its barest form: "A plot is the moving suspense of story from disequilibrium to resolution" (52; see also 64). Between the disequilibrium and the resolution is the turning of a "strange corner" (57) or the reversal in which "tables are turned, viewpoints are reversed" (73). In *The Homiletical Plot* (1980), Lowry's plot is amplified and more restrictive. Here "the homiletical plot" consists of five sections: the initial "upsetting the equilibrium"; "analyzing the discrepancy," or discovering the explanatory why; the reversal, turning point, or "disclosing the clue to resolution"; "experiencing the gospel"; and "anticipating the consequences." He lightheartedly labels these five "oops," "ugh," "aha," "whee," and "yeah" (25). In *How to Preach a Parable* (1989), Lowry equates the narrative form with a fourfold sequence: opening disequilibrium, escalation of conflict, surprising reversal, and closing denouement (25; see also 1990, 70). Elsewhere, he calls this fourfold pattern "the typical plot" (1985, 64). In its simplest form, however, "the process of narrativity" is the movement "from disequilibrium to resolution" (1989, 26). I believe this bare-bones plot provides the most room for constructing narrative sermons. A plot's critical ingredients are the disequilibrium and the resolution with the intervening turn toward resolution.

Lowry's terms for the opening disequilibrium include bind, itch, problem, imbalance, ambiguity, tension, incompleteness, conflict, discrepancy, and trouble (1980, 28–35; 1985, 53–56; 1989, 32–33). Of critical importance is that the conflict be "lived" (1985, 47), that the ambiguity or problem be "felt" (1980, 29, 30), that the trouble be so real that "one cannot breathe easily until some solution occurs" (1980, 29). "Something" is "at stake" (1985, 64) both for the preacher and the congregation. Lowry writes of preachers that "our sermonic itch must become theirs" (1980, 29), and "the ambiguity must be felt by the listeners, not just the preacher" (1980, 30; see also 1985, 24, 64).

A second key element in the narrative plot is the resolution. Lowry describes the resolution as "the underlying principle" for ordering a sermon as an experience or happening (1985, 20). In the resolution, "the table of life gets set for us in a new way by the gospel" (1989, 25) or life is put back together again (1985, 73). The resolution constitutes the change brought about by the gospel or the Word—the easing of tension, the reestablishment of equilibrium, the clarifying of ambiguity. And it is an experience, "both a knowing and a feeling" (1980, 29). Two further characteristics of the resolution are that it be "born of the gospel" (1985, 66) and that it be integral to the plot itself, "not tacked on" (1989, 140).

As with the disequilibrium, both the preacher and the congregation must share the resolution. The preacher is "the first recipient of the good news" (1989, 114). Lowry explains:

> If we expect our hearers to be changed by the Word, and if we presume that preaching may occasion such change, then we need to be ready for change ourselves. There is no way we can produce the change, but we do have the responsibility of doing those things which will place us in optimum position so that we may be changed by the power of the gospel. . . . And that means setting the stage for ourselves first before presuming to set it for anyone else. (1980, 86–87)

The final element I want to lift up from Lowry's discussions of the narrative plot as a sermonic form is the reversal, or turning point. Sometimes Lowry emphasizes "*the principle of reversal*" that "*turns things upside down*" (1980, 48, Lowry's italics; see also 60). The sermonic reversal is like "pulling the rug out from under someone" (1980, 56), a move that Lowry justifies by claiming that the gospel is experienced as "*radical discontinuity*" and "*inversion*" (1980, 60, Lowry's italics; see also 1985, 73). At other times Lowry is less insistent that the turning point be so radical or disruptive. After analyzing two jokes that illustrate the principle of reversal, he admits that "not every joke form contains as radical a reversal as the above two" (1980, 49):

It would be unreasonable to assume that Sunday after Sunday, the ordinary preacher is going to provide such dramatic, jolting, or funny reversals as I have just illustrated from plays and jokes. (1980, 51)

Then Lowry continues, "Nonetheless, the principle has validity and can be accomplished more easily than one might think" (1980, 51). However, Lowry opens the door to the possibility that the clue to resolution or the sermon's turning point might be more simply a sudden shift (1980, 49–50), a seeing of matters in a different light (1980, 46), or a finding of oneself (1985, 49).

For Lowry, the sermon's turning point comes from the preacher's wrestling with the text. And it comes as a surprise or a revelation for which the preacher must wait (1980, 84). Lowry describes the process hypothetically:

You begin sermon preparation on an Old Testament narrative. You already know what you're going to say—sort of. But then the passage begins leading you down a new road. Perhaps you are paraphrasing a scene out loud to yourself, and then you begin saying things and seeing things you'd never thought before. You are utterly surprised with it all and suddenly, . . . your new homiletical question is: How can I relive the experience in the pulpit in such a way that they can see and hear what I just saw and heard? (1985, 49).

Lowry and Craddock are both interested in the sermon's being an experience for the congregation, and they both advocate a sermonic form that aims to shape an experience for the congregation by recreating the preacher's interaction with a text. They differ, however, in that their processes for forming the sermon begin at opposite ends. Craddock starts with the end of the sermon, with the preacher's knowing the sermon's destination. The inductive preacher "re-creates the experience of arriving at a conclusion" (1974, 125). Lowry starts with the beginning of the sermon and encourages the preacher to be content "*not to know* the end product before one actually begins writing" (1985, 104). The narrative preacher belongs among those artists who "report how little they knew about a story's conclusion when they began writing" (16).

Transformational preaching represents a third voice at the homiletical table. While borrowing from one another, each voice represents distinctive views of preaching's whys, whats, and hows. Another way to imagine it is that traditional, kerygmatic, and transformational views of preaching are bands along a spectrum. Although the bands overlap and fade one into the next, each band is generally distinguishable by certain predominant characteristics. What distinguishes kerygmatic theory from traditional theory is largely a matter of new convictions about the purpose and content of preaching. What distinguishes transformational views of preaching from kerygmatic theory is largely a matter of new convictions about language and form.

Responding

I undertake a response to transformational understandings of preaching with some trepidation because for years I have found a home under this umbrella. My discovering these new directions in preaching in the mid–1980s felt like a homecoming, and I offer this response only with deep gratitude to these scholars who helped me find my voice as a preacher. I also recognize that I remain deeply influenced by transformational understandings of preaching. I have not abandoned many of these convictions and assumptions. My three responses here and my proposal for an additional understanding of preaching reflect the many ways my views overlap with transformational views of preaching even as they attempt to break new ground.

Response One: The Gap
Between Preacher and Congregation

A major issue with transformational understandings of preaching is that the gap between the preacher and the congregation remains. Therefore, these descriptions of preaching remain problematic for those of us who envision the preacher and the congregation as standing in solidarity one with the other. I will not repeat my previous critique of this gap. Instead, I will use the words of several transformational scholars to highlight the sense of separation that continues to set the preacher apart from the congregation. Then I will raise questions about sermonic efforts to transfer an experience from the preacher to the congregation.

Sometimes in discussions of transformational preaching the gap is explicit in the preacher's aggressive attitude toward the congregation. Riegert claims that the preacher must "un-arrange" and redesign the minds and lives of the worshipers (1990, 121, 134).

Sometimes the gap continues in echoes of traditional preaching's focus on transmission. Salmon defines "eucatastrophe" as the transforming, grace-filled experience of the gospel; it is "a positive upheaval, a marvelous inbreaking of blessing" (1988, 10). For Salmon, "preaching is essentially an effort to communicate, transmit, transfer that experience of eucatastrophe" (11). Here what is transmitted is no longer an idea or a message but a transforming experience. Other scholars express similar views. Long's preacher is a witness whose task is "to find just those words and patterns that can convey the event the witness has heard and seen" (1989b, 46).

The preacher remains in the privileged position of the one who has already experienced the transformation that the congregation now needs to experience. The congregation remains in the subordinate position of recipients whose options are rejecting or receiving those images and patterns, sights and sounds capable of effecting transformation. Transformational preaching remains essentially one-directional, crossing the gap from the pulpit to the pew.

The image of the sermon as conveying or transferring an experience, whether a word-event encoded in the text or the preacher's wrestling with a text, deserves further attention. Elisabeth Schüssler Fiorenza raises questions about this image of preaching (1983). She writes that both the sociology of knowledge and recent theological insight deny the existence of raw or uninterpreted experience (44). Every experience is particular and "shaped by its historical conditions in time and space, in culture and gender socialization" (44–45). Therefore, every experience of a text is particular to the interpreter and historically conditioned. Schüssler Fiorenza does not seek to break the link between preaching and each preacher's particular experiences; in fact, she claims the link is a given. Instead, she warns homilists not to present their own experiences as though they were "paradigmatic for Christian God-experience today" (44). In other words, both the preacher's personal wrestling with the text as well as any interpretation of the text's original or performative intention are particular experiences that bear the marks of the preacher's social, historical conditioning.

Schüssler Fiorenza raises her warning as "the proverbial 'woman in the pew,'" a member of "the silenced majority," who are still barred in many Christian churches "from *defining* the role of proclamation in terms of their own experience" (45). She contends:

> In such an ecclesiastical situation the danger exists that the homily will not articulate the experience of God as the rich and pluriform experience of God's people, but that the male preacher will articulate his own experience and will declare and proclaim his own particular experience as the experience of God *par excellence.* What is limited and particular to his experience will be proclaimed as universal and paradigmatic for everyone. [6]

The danger Schüssler Fiorenza raises is not limited to churches that exclude women preachers. The danger exists wherever preachers assume that their experiences of texts or their interpretations of what texts "say and do" are normative and then use the sermon as a vehicle to transfer those experiences to the congregation.

Walter Brueggemann similarly claims that interpretation is never "innocent or disinterested" (1988, 131). Every biblical text requires interpretation that always betrays the "vested interest" of the interpreters (130, 135, 144). Interpreters "always present reality in partisan ways and, indeed, cannot do otherwise" (137). Consequently, preaching, as an act of interpretation, "is never a benign, innocent, or straightforward act. Anyone who imagines that he or she is a benign or innocent preacher of the text is engaged in self-deception" (131). Thus, both the reading of texts—as a search for an encoded intentionality or as a personal wrestling—and the crafting of sermons reflect the preacher's self-interested particularity.

The implications of these claims by Schüssler Fiorenza and Brueggemann for sermon making are substantial. Few homiletical scholars expressly acknowledge the claim that the preacher's wrestling with or interpretation of a text is always particular, historically conditioned, and vested with self-interest. They assert or imply that something of the text is recoverable: for some, the author's intention; for others, the experience of God's Word behind or encoded in the text. For David Buttrick, the consciousness that the text intends to construct in its audience is available to the astute interpreter (1987). He is confident that "by spotting vocabulary, rhetorical strategies, and the like, in the Corinthian correspondence, we can construct an understanding of the world that must have been in the consciousness of the Corinthian congregation" (296–97).

Richard Lischer disagrees with these efforts at recovery and believes that "this side of mysticism, no amount of exegesis or homiletical technique will allow preacher and hearers to cross over into another time and into another person's skin. The otherness of the past remains" (1981, 89–90). Following Martin Luther, Lischer describes "the interpreter's distance from a true understanding of God's Word" that is the result of "human sinfulness and creatureliness" (89). Yet Lischer proposes that "preaching begins with hearing the voice of God" (91). Similarly, Long is confident that "the voice of Scripture" can be discerned, although "it is no easy task genuinely to listen to the voice of Scripture rather than merely to hear the sound of our own echoes" (1989a, 28). Neither Long nor Lischer raises the possibility that every encounter with "the voice of Scripture" (ibid.) or "the voice of God" (Lischer 1981, 91) is ambiguously mingled with "the sound of our own echoes" (Long 1989a, 28). Few homiletical scholars acknowledge as explicitly as Gardner Taylor that "the coloring and texturing of the sermon, no matter what the text may be, will be influenced by the personality and outlook of the preacher" (1983, 138).

Taylor's, Schüssler Fiorenza's, and Brueggemann's comments reflect a claim that some of us have believed for a long time, especially those of us who have lived and worked in a world that has only reluctantly made room for us and our different experiences, phenomenological narratives, and interpretations. Some of us are convinced that every reading of every text and every voice interpreted as belonging to God or Scripture is colored and textured by the personality, conditioned by the socialization, and vested with the interests of the interpreter.

In making this claim, my intention is not to single out scholars under the transformational umbrella as particularly culpable. My intention, instead, is to highlight a danger when this claim is ignored and to demonstrate the persistence of the gap. The danger, in Craddock's words, is "imperialism of thought and feeling" (1974, 65). Craddock's inductive method reflects his express effort to avoid such imperialism by giving the congregation "room to respond" (65). Yet his description of the difficult struggle to "resist the temptation to tyranny of ideas" (64) reflects a fundamental separation between the preacher and the congregation. The preacher who "wants to possess and control not only the subject but all who hear it" (64) demonstrates blatant separation. The preacher who resists the temptation and engages in "democratic sharing" (64) demonstrates a commitment to overcoming separation. In both cases, the fundamental experience is separation.

In transformational preaching, the gap remains as either an asset to be partially valued (Long 1989b, 131) or a liability to be overcome (Craddock 1974). The question consequently remains, What is preaching all about for those of us who are not particularly tempted by "imperialism of thought or feeling" (Craddock 1974, 65) because our fundamental experience is one of connectedness?

Response Two: Language

Schüssler Fiorenza's claim that experience is never pure but always historically conditioned (1983) lifts to the forefront a second problem. While discussions of transformational preaching presuppose the power of language to shape consciousness, they generally do not address the biased and limited nature of language that reflects its historical conditioning.

Most transformational scholars do not discuss the problem of the fallen nature of language in general. They reject scientific or descriptive language not because the bond by which words correspond to reality is unreliable or nonexistent. Instead, they base their rejection on the conviction that the language of one-to-one correspondence is inadequate "for enabling the mind and spirit to touch upon the profound, ever-elusive mysteries of existence" (Wardlaw 1983, 18). The conviction is not that all language is historically conditioned but that poetic language is preferable to scientific language, or that the performative function of language is preferable to its descriptive function. Poetic language is valued because it is deemed capable of connecting human existence with a reality that lies just beyond language, a Word or voice that seeks to come to expression in language. Performative language is valued because it is deemed capable of creating or evoking the reality to which it refers.

But what if all language is fallen, freighted, vested with the interests of its users? What if all language participates in the sinful distortions and the limitations of human existence and of particular human communities at particular periods of time? What if the preacher is an inescapable variable in the task of interpretation? Discussions of such possibilities by homiletical scholars are rare.

Clement Welsh introduces "linguistic relativity" into the homiletical conversation (1974). He ponders a "theory of 'linguistic relativity,'" proposed by Benjamin Lee Whorf (80). Whorf's hypothesis is "that since a language emerges within the culture of a certain people, and since their experience of the world is naturally limited, that language can only present a limited view of the universe" (80).[7] This theory disturbs Welsh who confesses that "the linguistic relativity hypothesis really pinches . . . if it suggests that one is imprisoned within his language so completely that it governs his perception of the universe and limits what he can know of it" (81). Allowing himself to feel the pinch, Welsh concedes that one's language invites some experiences and precludes others. He, therefore, expresses concern about the "unsuspected limitations" and the "discoverable relativism" of language (82).

For Robert E. C. Browne, the ambiguity of language is a given (1985). Because knowledge is limited, language can never be unequivocal, unambiguous, or more than a gesture. All statements are approximations:

> Modern scientists do not claim to be able to give a literal description of the universe; they will say that the most accurate measuring and weighing are no more than the nearest approximations. Poets hold that they never mean exactly what they say because they cannot say exactly what they mean. Artists explain that the painter cannot step out of a landscape and paint it as a detached spectator producing a picture which is to be marked correct or incorrect as a child's sum in arithmetic is marked. The statements made by a minister of the Word are as ambiguous as those made by artists and scientists whose work helps him to understand that all his doctrinal statements are approximate and untidy descriptions of reality. (70)

Like the painter who "cannot step out of a landscape and paint it as a detached spectator" (70), the preacher can never escape "the ways in which he is conditioned by the preoccupations of the society in whose life he participates" (93). The very language the preacher uses has been produced by a particular generation and reflects "its faith, its disbeliefs, its preoccupations, its anxieties, its achievements, its amusements, its hopes and its fears" (92).

Whereas Browne believes that words can be "approximate and untidy descriptions of reality" (70), Joseph Sittler seriously questions the correspondence between words and reality (1966, 48, 51). Sittler's concern, however, is broader than language. It also includes "musical grammar" and "architectural grammar" (47). His argument is that language, music, and architecture no longer express and celebrate a consensus about the nature of reality. He contrasts the eighteenth-century music of George Frederick Handel with the modern music of Thelonious Monk. Handel's music reflected "the clear realities of his world" because of "an agreed consensus about the world" (50). Or more precisely, Handel's music expressed "the measured, confident, ordered world of political and social life in upper class England, Austria, France, colonial America" (49). Sittler identifies Handel's music as "the outer and audible noise of an inward and secure world of one class at one place for a certain period" (49). Monk's music reflects a world in which "reality is in transit" (50). Therefore "Monk has no choice but to construct and impose upon life however strange and arbitrary his work may sound, his *own* reality—which is for him the only one there is" (50). Modern artists, Sittler claims, create by bestowing or imposing a form on what they see and handle (54) because no consensus dictates agreed-upon convictions about the nature of reality.

For Sittler, language is "one of [our] most venerable 'forming' activities'"(53); it is "the grammar of our beholding minds" (51). And the revolutionary discovery of the second half of the twentieth century is that this grammar that shapes our thinking and seeing may not correspond to the way things are (51). Sittler is unclear as to whether "the nature of the reality of things themselves is now searching for a vocabulary" (49) or whether, like Handel's and Monk's music, language is an arbitrary form conferred upon reality and representing a particular view of the world by one artist or one class in one geographical region for a certain period of time.

Sometimes Sittler seems to come close to Browne's conception of language as "approximate and untidy descriptions of reality" (1958, 70). He hopes for "a fresh apprehension of reality " (55) and has confidence in "the inner nature of things" (60). For Sittler, realities have power to work in the world, evoking and creating beauty and grace (65). In some approximate way, language seeks to reveal and celebrate reality.

At other times Sittler seems to be making a more radical claim. For example, he discusses form, which includes language, in the context of science's procedural models for which investigators "claim nothing philosophical or objectively verifiable at all" (51). He argues that the Christian faith is not verifiable on "trans-historical" grounds, "either ontological or existential" (63). Thus he severs the language of faith from any fixed or indisputable correspondence to reality. And he implies that the language of faith, because it is a form, is "a convenient order" (49) bestowed on the disorder of the world by the community of faith. Moreover, he draws a parallel between the artist who imposes a new reality on "the shattered world-understanding" and the contemporary theologian who seeks "to explicate the meaning of God and [humanity] and the world out of the historical particularity of the terms, episodes, patterns of the biblical story" (62). The implication is that language as a human form imposes a certain order on reality that reflects the consensus of a particular people at a particular point in time.

Does language then reflect an order inherent in the nature of reality, or does it impose a particular, limited order on reality? I prefer to live with the ambiguity and tension that Sittler raises.[8]

Language is powerful. It can create new worlds in consciousness. But it is also limited and participates in the sins and distortions of the generations and cultures that use and reshape it. This conviction about the limited nature of language, for me, pushes considerations of preaching beyond the views of transformational preaching. The claim that all language is irrevocably biased precludes the preacher's discovering an intention, voice, or experience that purports to be the text's intention, the voice of God, or a paradigmatic gospel experience.

Response Three: The Sermon
as Agent of Change

A third response to transformational views of preaching is that, on the one hand, they continue the problem created when the sermon is envisioned as an every-week event, and, on the other hand, they create a new problem by claiming that the sermonic event should change the worshiping congregation. Since I have already discussed the problem of the sermon's being an event, I will address here only this new problem.

Some homiletical scholars recognize that to expect a sermon consistently to change people may be expecting too much. And a number of scholars admit that preaching does a poor job of changing lives. Riegert, a staunch advocate of preaching as transforming event, acknowledges the charge:

> It is salutary to remind ourselves that in the tortured and exuberant decade of the 1960s some voices flatly claimed preachers should give [up] expecting sermons to effect change. Clyde Reid's was one of the sharpest. Preaching, he argued, could do many things: give information, inspire, comfort and strengthen, challenge with a new vision, reinforce attitudes and beliefs already held. And most of these it could do rather well—especially the reinforcement of attitudes and beliefs already held by the hearers. *But preaching could not effect change.* On that point Reid was adamant and remorseless. (1990, 19, Riegert's italics)

J. Randall Nichols also discusses the charge that preaching does a poor job of changing people (1987). Like Riegert, he then reaffirms his conviction that preaching should change people and suggests more effective strategies (57).

The Bishops' Committee on Priestly Life and Ministry, however, claims that preaching should not aim "to bring about a change in attitude or behavior" (1982, 26). Its members base their claim on the evidence of social science research, which suggests "that the oral presentation of a single person is not particularly effective" in effecting change (26). Then they redescribe preaching in ways that move beyond transformational views.

Should preaching seek to transform the congregation week after week? A "no" answer arises from a different direction. Many transformational discussions of preaching are rooted in a particular branch of parable studies and shifting definitions of a parable.[9] In the homiletical literature, when a parable is defined as an illustration or explanation of a truth, traditional and kerygmatic theories of preaching hold. But when the parable is defined as the vehicle for an imaginative reversal that takes place in the consciousness of those to whom it is addressed, transformational views of preaching arise. For some transformational scholars, the sermon, like the parable, should shake the congregation loose from established ways of being in the world and create new ways more consistent with the gospel. Riegert, for example, claims that preaching "shatters conventional reality" and "discloses the world of *God's* reality" (1990, 14).

Such preaching is an invitation to the congregation *"to live in the world it has disclosed"* (110, Riegert's italics).

The question, Should every sermon seek to transform the congregation? could be rephrased, Should every sermon function like a parable? Browne (1958) indirectly says "No." He quotes T. S. Eliot, "It would not be desirable, even if it were possible, to live in a state of perpetual revolution."[10] Here I take issue with those who seem to imply that preaching should always be replacing worldviews, reversing attitudes, or opening up new worlds of consciousness. Some discussions of transformational preaching leave the impression that the preacher and the congregation should be in a state of perpetual transformation.

Preaching sometimes is transformative. It sometimes converts; it sometimes nudges believers in saving, sanctifying directions. My concern is not whether a sermon on occasion *does* transform but whether every sermon *should seek*, as its primary goal, to transform the congregation week after week.

I am deeply indebted to transformational views of preaching. They have been my springboard for developing a preaching style more consistent with my deepest convictions and experiences. My own proposal clearly builds on, even while it seeks to push beyond, transformational understandings of preaching.

from *A Way of Staying Sane*

Maxine Kumin

I write these poems because I have to. I wrestle with my own notions of human depravity in this, and in other poems, not because I think the poem can change our foreign policy, soften the heart of the military-industrial complex that feeds on first-strike potential propaganda, or arouse the citizenry to acts of civil disobedience for peace, but because, for my own sanity (and yours, and yours), I must live the dream out to the end. It is important to act as if bearing witness matters. To write about the monstrous sense of alienation the poet feels in this culture of polarized hatreds is a way of staying sane. With the poem, I reach out to an audience equally at odds with official policy, and I celebrate our mutual humanness in an inhuman world.

4 ∽ *Marginal Voices*
Crowd Around the Table

What is preaching all about when the preacher and the congregation experience "connection and solidarity" (Smith 1989, 48) as their primary relationship? This question arises from preachers who assume that the worshipers are their partners in matters of faith and practice. It also arises from members of worshiping communities who accept responsibility for being interpreters of life and faith, accountable in these areas to God, one another, and the larger household of faith. Marginal voices enter the homiletical conversation because the three dominant views of preaching leave this question unexplored.

Two Preliminary Convictions

Two basic convictions or presuppositions undergird my explorations of an alternative understanding of preaching. One concerns the relationship between the preacher and the congregation as equal partners on a journey to understand and live out their faith commitments. A second concerns the limitations and sinfulness of language.

The Partnership Between
Preacher and Congregation

Fundamental to my experiences of and reflections on preaching is the conviction that the preacher and congregation are not separate entities but a community of faith. My experiences of preaching are rooted in connectedness and solidarity, which stand at the opposite end of a spectrum from separation and distance. My life experiences offer insight into both ends of the spectrum. At times I find myself in circumstances that emphasize the differences between me and those around me. I therefore shape my behavior in accordance with these differences or the gulf that separates me from these others. In such circumstances my mode of relating often evidences varying degrees of defensiveness. At some extreme end of this experience of separation is Jean-François Lyotard's claim, "To speak is to fight" (Lyotard 1984, 10). At other times I find myself in circumstances that emphasize the similarities between me and those around me, or I am in a group that is inseparable from a fundamental sense of who I am. One such group is my family. Another is the church, as particular congregations and more generally as the inclusive household or family of

God. In such circumstances I shape my behavior in accordance with a sense
of solidarity, equality, and mutuality by which we are bound together. At some
extreme end of this experience of connectedness is co-dependency that blurs
the boundaries separating one's self from others.

Even as I recognize both ends of the spectrum, I believe I do not function well
in settings that highlight separation because my primary mode of being is rooted
in a sense of connectedness. Feminist scholarship suggests that either connectedness or separation characterizes a person's fundamental life experiences.

According to feminist scholarship, the primary mode of relating for many men
is based on a sense of separation from others. For some of these men, intimacy
and community are threats to autonomy; for others, they are highly prized values toward which they strive. Feminist scholarship also claims that the primary
mode of relating for many women is based on a sense of connectedness. For
some of these women, separation from others is feared as debilitating isolation;
for others, it is cultivated as the handmaiden of individuation.

The dominant understandings of preaching, presupposing a gap between
the preacher and the congregation, are rooted in separation. Even those scholars who image the preacher and the congregation as standing together continue
to describe preaching as though the preacher had an idea, gospel message, or
experience to communicate or transfer to the congregation. If the preacher's
task is to teach, persuade, or change the congregation, the preacher and the
congregation stand apart from each other. Thus the preacher and the congregation remain separate, even while community and shared life are affirmed.

The experience of many of us in both the pulpit and the pew is that we are
interdependent, not separated by a gap but joined in common discipleship and
common tasks. For us the gap shifts. The preacher and the congregation stand
together as explorers, while a text, meaning, or mystery lies on the other side
or confronts us as Other. Thus situated, we as preachers have no message,
gospel, or experience for the congregation to receive. In the pulpit we are not
senders, and in the pew we are not receivers. The fundamental experience of
connectedness redescribes the roles of the preacher and the worshipers and
demands new probes into preaching's whys, whats, and hows.

The Limitations
of Language

A second conviction that undergirds my proposal for an additional understanding of preaching is that all language, including the language of faith, is
inevitably biased and limited, historically conditioned, and inseparable from
the sins of each generation and each community of users. Here I want briefly
to revisit Browne and Sittler.

Browne describes "the ambiguity inherent in all use of language" (1958, 73).
Words are not so linked to unchanging entities that we can point to something

explicit "and say, 'When I use this word that is exactly what I mean, no more and no less'" (65). Linguistic ambiguity is inevitable; "silence would be the only way to avoid ambiguity in speech" (66). Why is linguistic ambiguity inevitable? Browne answers, because human knowledge is fragmentary and inexact (40, 48, 73, 112), because as human beings we are both limited creatures and sinners (22, 48), and because we are "conditioned by the preoccupations of the society" in which we participate (93, see 92).

For Browne, however, linguistic ambiguity does not preclude the possibility of knowledge (39). Knowledge simply "cannot be communicated in unequivocal terms" (94). Likewise for Browne, linguistic ambiguity does not mean that preachers cannot "speak the truth" (25). Any truth they speak, however, will always remain ambiguous:

> Christians are taught to say that God is our father and the phrase is taught on the highest authority. It is right that we should speak of God as a person, for person is the name of the highest kind of life we know. But by speaking of God as a person we have not made a definition. We do not know fully what we mean by the word *person*; it is the word we use to signify our limited knowledge of what it means to be human. (43)

Browne continues, when we say "God is a person," we are not stating "a simple equation" because we are "dealing with two partially unknowns" (43). If we circumvent "this difficulty by selecting a definition of *person*," the result is we get "no more out of the equation than [we have] put into it" (43). We "cannot prove [our] answer, for God continues to be not fully knowable" (43).

Joseph Sittler is another homiletical scholar who believes that language reflects the particularities of the historical, social, and political world to which it belongs (1966). For Sittler, no facile correspondence exists between reality and the language which constructs it and seeks to reflect it. This awareness of the "the limits of [the mind's] correspondence to reality" (55) constitutes a "revolution in our apprehension of the world," a revolution that is "*vital* and *absolute*" (48). At the same time, Sittler believes that divine reality is active in human experience: God continues to liberate people in human history; Christ remains a presence who can be trusted; and the Holy Spirit continues to shape and sustain the community of believers (63).

These two convictions—that the preacher and the worshipers are equal partners on a journey to understand and live out their faith commitments, and that language, including the language of faith, is never innocent or unambiguous—undergird this proposal for a new voice at the homiletical table.

Rethinking Preaching's Why

My understanding of preaching's purpose builds on the groundwork laid by Browne (1958), who both created space for me to question the dominant understandings and set me on the road to articulating my own.

According to Browne, preaching's aim is not to transmit a message, a claim of traditional and kerygmatic preaching. Browne's argument here is that a sermon is like a poem (23):

> Unlike an advertisement, a poem or a sermon does not try to impose something on those who pay attention. Poets and preachers cannot predict or control the response that people make to their utterances; to make a poem or a sermon is to give it a life of its own. . . . The sermon's existence is somewhere between the preacher and the members of the congregation; it has a reality which is not simply the reality of what the preacher is trying to express. (29)

Nor is preaching's aim to replicate a prior experience, a claim of transformational views of preaching. Browne claims that no sermon can recreate an experience because to recollect and describe any experience in fact creates a new one (28–29).

Browne proposes instead that preaching should aim to show people how to make sense of their lives.[1] Each sermon should be an honest attempt to interpret life experiences. What is important is not the congregation's believing the preacher's interpretation but their recognizing that for the preacher the interpretation is genuine (77–78). For Browne, the sermon should communicate not the results of the preacher's thinking but a process of thinking that enables the members of the congregation to understand themselves and their lives more clearly (77, 97).

Browne's view of preaching's purpose reenvisions the roles of the preacher and the congregation. The preacher is not an answer-person. Final answers are not the result of either preaching or doctrine. Doctrine, Browne explains, is not "the answer to every question but the way to begin answering; doctrine does not tell a [person] what to think but how to think" (47). Instead of being answer-persons, preachers become "living agent[s] in the process of enlarging [their] hearers' understanding of themselves" (77). This process involves the interpretation of "life in terms of doctrine and doctrine in terms of life" (52). Through preaching, the people learn to participate in this interpretive process.

My discomfort with Browne's descriptions of preaching's purpose focuses primarily on the gap that continues to separate the congregation and the preacher. Preaching remains one-directional in that the sermon's goal is to enlarge (77) the people by communicating a process the preacher already understands. Browne's preacher remains too solitary, too much the director in preaching, too little a partner among equals.

Browne does succeed, however, in offering a description of preaching's purpose distinct from the dominant views. He proposes that preaching's aim is to nurture a process whereby worshipers take responsibility for making sense of their own lives. Browne's alternative to the dominant views of preaching's purpose sparked my own rethinking. His image of preaching as nurturing a process forms the basis for my own proposal.

I propose that one form of preaching aims to gather the community of faith around the Word where the central conversations of the people of God are fostered and refocused week after week. I am calling this proposal a conversational understanding of preaching. Underlying this proposal is the experience of solidarity already present in the preaching moment for some preachers and worshipers. The various components of this proposal build on insights and hints I have gleaned from listening to my homiletical colleagues.

At the heart of my proposal is the idea that preaching gathers the community of faith around the Word. Dietrich Ritschl introduces the image of preaching as a gathering activity (1960). He writes, "Preaching is not dispensing power or giving something to people, but preaching is receiving power and collecting and gathering people" (22). The power that gathers the people of God and the center that continues to sustain and shape the community of faith is the Word.

For Ritschl, in this community gathered by and living "under the Word" (155), any gap between the preacher and the congregation is cruel, self-inflicted, and unnecessary. He writes that "part of the cruelty (which we ourselves have created) of our Church is that minister and congregation are separated in such a way that the preacher is alone and isolated with [the] preaching task" (15–16). He believes that the preacher and the congregation share in the priesthood of all believers. Rightly understood, this doctrine means that edification is the responsibility of all members of the congregation (122). Members are given gifts, *charismata,* for the edification of others (122). Thus, all ministry, including preaching (33), becomes the joint task of the preacher and the congregation.

In pursuing their shared priesthood, the preacher and the people together seek to interpret the Word. Instead of preachers being "alone and isolated," studying and making interpretive decisions apart from the people (124), Ritschl urges them to join the congregation for pre-sermon Bible study where they share the results of private biblical study with the people, where they raise questions, suggest answers, and receive from the people new questions and answers (155).[2] Ritschl here describes a mutual sharing in which all participants raise questions, propose answers, and remain open to further questions and answers from one another. In such a context, preachers are not the sole teachers or the "celebrated" theologians (155); nor are they seeking ways to package in convincing ways previously conceived messages. Instead, preachers and people become brothers and sisters "under the Word" (155) so that discerning the Word of God becomes a joint task.

Furthermore, for Ritschl, members of the community have an additional responsibility for preaching as they proclaim the gospel during the week. Their proclamation is not distinct from the preacher's (126). Preaching as the responsibility of the entire church (33) unites the preacher and the people in shared ministry.

Ritschl's predominant belief about preaching's purpose never moves beyond kerygmatic theory: preaching is so to proclaim the Word that Jesus Christ
becomes the "true Preacher" (20, 22, 108; see also 33, 45). At the same time,
hints emerge of a new understanding of preaching's purpose—gathering the
community of faith around the Word. Seeking to undermine any gap between
the preacher and the congregation, Ritschl describes preaching as belonging
to all the worshipers, all of whom have gifts for "mutual edification" (122). This
understanding of preaching implies a nonhierarchical understanding of the
church that is grounded in the priesthood of all believers and in life lived in
partnership under the Word.

One component of my proposal is this gathering of the people of God
around the Word. A second component is that conversational preaching fosters and refocuses the church's central conversations. The concept of preaching as a conversation in the context of ongoing conversations is not new.

Joseph Fichtner begins *To Stand and Preach for Christ: A Theology of
Preaching* by describing preaching as "the conversation of the Christian life"
whose main topic is God and humanity's relationship to God (1981, v).[3] Toward the end of his book he again links the homily and conversation. The
Greek word *homily* means "familiar conversation" similar to the exchange of
the two apostles on the road to Emmaus, as they talked "with each other about
all these things that had happened" (124). Fichtner adds that preachers should
not be startled if the congregation answers back and begins a dialogue (124).
For Fichtner, the conversation that is preaching includes more than the
preacher and the congregation. Because Fichtner's view of preaching is kerygmatic, God is not only preaching's topic but also an active participant.

The Bishops' Committee on Priestly Life and Ministry also discusses preaching as a conversation between the preacher and the congregation (1982). Its
members cite two biblical instances where the verb for *homily* means "engaged
in conversation": the exchange between the disciples on the way to Emmaus
in Luke 24:14 and the exchange between Antonius Felix, Procurator of Judea,
and Paul in Acts 24:26 (24). From this evidence they conclude that the homily
should be "more like a personal conversation, albeit a conversation on matters of utmost importance, than like a speech or classroom lecture" (24). The
goal of such a conversation is not to impart new information or to change attitudes or behavior but "to make explicit or to reinforce attitudes or knowledge
previously held" (26).

According to the Bishops' Committee, the congregation and the preacher share
a common identity as believers. Some level of faith on the part of the congregation can be assumed because they have gathered to worship (6, 17). The faith of
the preacher is also important. When parishioners were asked in a survey what
they hoped to experience during a sermon, they answered "simply to hear a person of faith speaking" (15). The image of preaching here is of one believer speaking conversationally among other believers in order to articulate or reinforce faith.

George W. Swank describes a similar view of preaching that makes "room for conversation" and fosters communal "reasoning together" (1981, 23). His is a "dialogic style" of preaching (20).[4] In language reminiscent of Browne, Swank suggests that the preacher should aim "to help the people think together, realizing that it is not necessary that they all come to the same opinion" (21–22). Such preaching "becomes part of a continuing conversation [between the preacher and the congregation] which started well before the preacher went to the pulpit, and which continues after the benediction" (57).

Swank envisions preaching as a conversation between "potential equals" (45). The worshipers are "colleagues from whom the speaker came and to whom the speaker will return" (21). Swank criticizes those preachers who consider the congregation to be "a collection of immature Christians who need to be straightened out" (45). If they are immature, Swank argues, they have the responsibility to examine and sort out their own lives (45).

This dialogic understanding of preaching, Swank claims, has historical precedents in Jewish sermons of the first several centuries B.C.E. These sermons were participatory, marked by questions, laughter, rude comments, and other interruptions (46–47). Swank also argues that sermons recorded in the Greek Testament were like disputes. His evidence is the dialogical pattern of sermons in Luke and especially Acts (48–49). Swank concludes: "From the beginning preaching was thus seen as an activity involving the whole people; it was the business of all who were present" (49).

Elisabeth Schüssler Fiorenza also contributes to this redescription of preaching as a conversation between the preacher and the congregation (1983). She calls for sermons that reflect the variety among the people of God who sit in the pews. Since homilists inevitably speak from the perspective of their personal experience and faith and since she has felt excluded from countless sermons, she urges homilists "to articulate publicly the learning processes and the experiences of the people of God as well,"[5] particularly, women,[6] the poor, and the disadvantaged (44–47). She is insistent that "it is only by taking seriously those interpretations that conflict with one's own theological and social presuppositions and conditions that the homilist is capable of broadening out the experiential and interpretative basis of proclamation" (52).[7] Preaching that reflects "the diversified experiences" of God's people (49) invites a broad spectrum of worshipers into the sermonic conversation.

These scholars both explicitly and implicitly develop the image of preaching as a conversation between the preacher and the congregation. In conversational preaching, this sermonic conversation is grounded in solidarity—a shared identity as the believing people of God, a shared priesthood before God and within community, and shared tasks of discerning and proclaiming God's Word.

In discussing preaching as a conversation between the preacher and the congregation, I do not mean to imply that other worshipers besides the preacher should speak during the time set aside in a service of worship for the sermon. Conversational sermons are not "dialogue sermons" or "interactive sermons," although these forms might lend themselves to conversational preaching. Instead, conversational preaching in part grows out of and reflects the ongoing conversations between the preacher and members of the congregation in which the preacher is not the one-in-the-know but an equal colleague in matters of living and believing. Instead of impeding these conversations with a final or single answer, the preacher fosters them by explicitly acknowledging a variety of points of view, learning processes, interpretations, and life experiences.

Other scholars expand the concept of preaching as conversation. Michael Schmaus suggests that the church should preach to itself (1966). He discusses preaching as a responsibility given to the entire church in baptism. Therefore, "everyone is called on to listen seriously to what a brother or sister says in all seriousness" (82). As the church thus preaches to itself, reforms arise "from various quarters" (82–83). In addition to preaching's role in reforming the church, "in our pluralist world, the preaching of the Church helps in orientation, clarification, encouragement, discrimination and direction finding" (98).

This dynamic interaction within the church informs Schmaus's understanding of preaching's purpose. He writes:

> When the aim of preaching is this relationship of the Church with itself—that is, the *Church's encounter with itself*—the preaching spreads outward within the compass of the inner circle, so that one person preaches to another and one group to another within the Church. In this situation, of course, the same person is not always the preacher, nor the same person always the listener. (96, Schmaus's italics)

Preaching's purpose involves fostering this encounter of the church "with itself" (96).

What are the central conversations that conversational preaching fosters? Various configurations include those between the preacher and the congregation, those within the church and its various constituencies (Schmaus 1966), those between the people and the Word (Ritschl 1960), and the trifold conversation among the preacher, the congregation, and God (Fichtner 1981).

Walter Brueggemann (1989) discusses preaching at the convergence of three conversations: one between the congregation and God; a second between preaching and the text; and a third between the preacher and the congregation (76). For Brueggemann, an important function of preaching is to reawaken speech wherever silence has stopped the life-giving conversation with God (49–50, 75–77). In a footnote to this discussion Brueggemann writes, "Much of the effort of liberation theology is concerned with the recovery of speech among the silenced and muted" (150).

The central ecclesial conversations in which preaching participates are multiple and layered. John S. McClure calls the congregation "a web of conversations" (1995, 57). On the one hand are the divine-human conversations in which the divine partner is God or the Word as found in its complexity and variety most fully in biblical texts. On the other hand are the human-human conversations within the particular community of faith, among communities of faith, between the dominant voices and those that are marginal and muted, and between the church and the world. Through the Spirit sometimes God becomes a participant in these human-human conversations, much as Jesus after the resurrection joined the two disciples as they "homilied" together on the road to Emmaus (Luke 24:13–15). In fostering all these conversations, of utmost importance is preaching's deliberate acknowledgment of the excluded voices of women, the poor, the disenfranchised (Schüssler Fiorenza 1983, 44–47), and "the silenced" (Brueggemann 1989, 150).

When preaching's goal is thus to gather the community of faith around the Word where the central conversations of the people of God are fostered and refocused week after week, new power arrangements emerge. That power is differently configured in conversational preaching has been implicit thus far in my discussion. Four scholars bring this issue explicitly into the homiletical conversation.

Schüssler Fiorenza proposes that the clergy should relinquish their monopoly of the pulpit, since the right to preach derives from baptism and from each believer's experiences of God (1983, 48, 55). Instead of equating their status as clergy with their role as preacher, the clergy should reinterpret their responsibility as ensuring that preaching occurs and then encourage and equip the laity to preach (48–49, 55).

Christine M. Smith also reimages the relationship between power and preaching (1989). She rejects any link between the preacher's authority and the capacity to influence or transform (46). Instead, for her, both authority and the power to transform belong to the community (47, 52). The preacher should not aim to transform the congregation, but the Christian community should aim to transform society. Within the community of faith, preaching is rooted in mutuality, equality, connectedness, and intimacy. Such preaching allows "each person in the community to do her or his own searching, struggling, celebrating, and naming" (57). However, Smith recognizes that women have long been silenced in the church and in society. Therefore preaching should give a privileged place to women's stories and experiences, as well as to their power to name (99).

A third reevaluation of the relationship between preaching and power is offered by Thomas J. Mickey.[8] Preaching, he claims, involves power because it participates in expressing, defining, and creating the community's identity and social order. In his new paradigm for preaching, these tasks belong to the entire congregation, not primarily to the preacher. Preaching's goal within a community of equals is to facilitate the communal tasks of defining, maintaining, and reforming corporate identity and social order.

Finally, McClure discusses the link between preaching and leadership (1995). His collaborative model of preaching presupposes shared power, which allows "all members of a community, from the center to the margins" "to participate in the interpretation of the community's mission and in decision-making" (21).

In a conversational view of preaching, the gathered community of faith is more than a collection of individuals; it also has a corporate identity and way of ordering its life. Conversational preaching, more than addressing an individual message to individual believers, is also concerned with "the formation and development of the Church" (Brown 1983, 70), with the upbuilding of the church as a people charged with the tasks of mutual edification and shared decision making. An emphasis on building up the church is not uncommon in discussions of traditional preaching where instruction is an important element in preaching. It is missing in most discussions of kerygmatic theory, which emphasizes the individual's encounter with God, and in discussions of transformational theory when the emphasis falls on the individual's experience of transformation.[9] The shift in conversational preaching is from the preacher's responsibility for upbuilding the church by providing answers or truths to the community's responsibility for its own formation and reformation.

Summary

What is preaching all about if its goal is not the transmission of truth, an encounter with God, or congregational transformation? Preaching's aim is week after week to gather the community of faith around the Word in order to foster and refocus its central conversations. Here preaching is about "mutual edification" (Ritschl 1960, 122) and mutual "orientation, clarification, encouragement, discrimination and direction-finding" (Schmaus 1966, 98). Here preaching is about the church's upbuilding itself as a priesthood of believers. Perhaps in a particular sermon the values of the particular congregation as it seeks to live in accordance with the gospel are reaffirmed and revalidated. Yet the partners in the conversations include God, the church in its various configurations, the marginal, the silenced, and the world. Therefore transformation or reformation is never excluded as a possible consequence of preaching. Transformation, however, is not a mark of successful preaching but the work of the Holy Spirit, which blows where it wills (John 3:8). In addition, the partners in the conversation include the gathered company of believers, biblical texts, and historical faith communities. Therefore transmission of the church's faith is unavoidable as the cumulative effect of preaching. In conversational preaching, however, the primary purpose of preaching is to gather worshipers regularly around the Word, to set texts and interpretations loose in the midst of the community, so that the essential conversations of God's people are nurtured.

This rethinking of preaching's purpose seeks to address three concerns raised by my earlier responses to the dominant voices in the homiletical conversation. First, whereas all three dominant descriptions of preaching's purpose presuppose a gap that separates the preacher and the congregation, conversational preaching begins in an experience of connectedness. A second concern was kerygmatic and transformational preaching's predominant focus on the sermon's effects on the individual believer. Conversational preaching, while not ignoring the individual, highlights the gathered community and its place within the people of God and the world. And, third, the expectation that the sermon should be an every-Sunday event or should continually transform people is too grand and leaves many preachers and congregations disappointed. A conversational understanding of preaching's purpose describes what may be happening in the church "when nothing seems to be happening in the affairs of faith" (Bartlett 1962, 98): a community of faith is gathering around the Word and refocusing its central conversations.

This description of the why of preaching combines with new understandings of the whats and hows of preaching to represent an additional voice at the homiletical table.

Rethinking Preaching's What

Three questions guide my rethinking of preaching's content. The first is, What is the content of preaching, given the limitations and biases of language? In other words, if no undistorted truth or fixed formulation of the gospel exists and if the recovery of a text's original meaning, the intention of its author, or an unbiased performance of the text is an impossibility, what do preachers preach? The second question is, Are words like *revelation, Word, kerygma,* and *truth* still useful in discussing the content of preaching? And finally, In the absence of certainty about truth, the gospel, or the meaning of texts, are there any controls over preaching's content?

Once again Browne (1958) inspired my rethinking. Browne bases his understanding of preaching's content on the presupposition that all human knowledge is limited and uncertain and that all human beings, though created in the image of God, are always limited and sinful (22). This presupposition affects his understanding of revelation and truth. If all human knowledge is inexact and incomplete, revelation is incomplete and inconclusive. In addition, revelation must always be expressed in cultural terms and reassimilated in each generation (92). Thus the truth of the Gospel, as the content of revelation, remains fragmentary, uncertain, and approximate. Revelation is also incomplete and uncertain because God is finally ineffable (27, see 43). Human speech about God is a "gesture" toward God (30), never a formula delimiting God. Only God lives in certainty and understands the totality of meaning (32, 43, 59). Humans must learn to live with the uncertainty of limited knowledge and fragmented truth (32, 39–40, 73, 127).

What then is preaching's content? Browne lays aside previous answers. His preacher is not interested in answers. Nor is his preacher interested in un-equivocal formulas (69, 77, 94); if the content of preaching could be reduced to a formula, "then there would be no need to make sermons" (77). Instead, Browne's preacher must live with an untidy mind on the fringes of error and resist fixed conclusions.

What then is preaching's content? Preaching offers interpretations of life (77) as "tentative judgments" (54; see 57, 59, 113) or "tentative conclusions" (113). For some, Browne acknowledges, such preaching might offer "too little to live on" (40). But, he claims, despite the fragmentation and uncertainty of human knowledge, revelation, and truth, what Christians have is enough to make life "bearable" and to make "significant living possible" (34, see 47–48).

Once again my proposal builds on Browne's. Preaching is about tentative interpretations, proposals that invite counterproposals, and the preacher's wa-gers as genuine convictions placed in conversation with the wagers of others. Each of these three words—*interpretation, proposal,* and *wager*—deserves consideration.

My first suggestion is that preaching's content consists of tentative interpre-tations—interpretations of life according to Browne and of biblical texts ac-cording to Walter Brueggemann. Why are they tentative? Because, Browne ar-gues, as fragments of the truth, they are limited and incomplete. Brueggemann argues differently (1988). He insists that no interpretation is "benign, innocent, or straightforward" (131). "The coming of the Enlightenment and the rise of modernity" gave rise to a "fascination with so-called objectivity," which in turn "led to the mistaken notion that reality did not need to be interpreted. As re-ality did not need to be interpreted, it was mistakenly concluded that the bib-lical text could be read in a straightforward manner without interpretation" (135–36). But, Brueggemann insists, every text requires interpretation, and every interpretation betrays the "vested interest" of the interpreters (130, 135, 144). In other words, interpreters, including preachers, "always present reality in partisan ways and, indeed, cannot do otherwise" (137). Preaching is about interpretations of life and texts; they are tentative because they are inescapably limited and self-interested.

A second word for preaching's content is *proposal,* a word I borrow from *Biblical Preaching on the Death of Jesus* (Beardslee and others 1989). Like Browne and Brueggemann, the authors of this book discuss preaching's con-tent within the context of the unavailability of absolute truth. They claim that the search for absolutes, for "that [which] stands beyond all relativity," is mis-taken (41). Truth belongs only to God who "knows all things as they truly are" (57). Human thought can never approximate God's truth in any quantitative way, "since our approximation to infinity is trivial" and human knowledge is always "fragmentary" and "remote" (57). Human thought can only approximate God's truth in a qualitative way, that is, by trying to be like God who is "all-inclusive and impartial" (59). To approach truth in this way requires confession and risk:

> We who are white are blind to the experience of those who are black or Hispanic. We who are male have not understood the world of female experience. . . . For the male, to become aware of female experience is to become aware that male experience is not only limited but also distorted, that even the finest ideals it has generated are frequently oppressive to women. This realization of Truth does not immediately suggest solutions, but it does demand the risk of untried alternatives. (60)

Determining preaching's content, therefore, is difficult because of human diversity. What might be liberating to one set of worshipers, say, men, might be oppressive to another, say, women (36, 134). In the absence of absolute truth and in the face of diversity, preaching's content is a "proposal" (36) or a "suggestion" (36) that invites the congregation's "collective response" (37).

The third key word in my proposal about preaching's content is *wager*.[10] Helmut Thielicke challenges preachers to proclaim that which deeply informs their living (1965, 5–11), that about which they are so convinced that they are willing "to advocate it as the 'truth'"(3). Thielicke's hope is that a preacher who proclaims such "truth" "really 'exists' in the house of" those truths (5). I suggest that when preachers do "exist" in this faith-house about which they preach, when they preach from the depths of their experiences and convictions, then their preaching is about wagers, those convictions upon which they have staked their lives or those insights where their journey has found a temporary resting-place. These wagers they now offer to others in the conversation called preaching, publicly acknowledging that their own personal wagers are particular and limited.

This understanding of preaching's content as partisan, tentative interpretations, as proposals that invite other proposals, as personal wagers aware of alternative wagers, assumes shifts in understandings of the terms *revelation, Word, kerygma,* and *truth.*

Edward Schillebeeckx suggests a reinterpretation of the concept of revelation (1964) that supports conversational preaching. He proposes that revelation is a dialogue (256–57, 270)—a dynamic, ongoing exchange that always requires interpretation and reinterpretation (256–57). Revelation is therefore always historically conditioned—the general dialogue between God and humanity in nature and history, as well as the Word of God as Christ, whose humanity is historically conditioned (257–58). Schillebeeckx reenvisions revelation as a "*special* conversation" (257) between God and humans.

Brueggemann further reinterprets this concept of the divine-human conversation (1989). Schillebeeckx recognizes that in both human-human conversations and the divine-human conversation the human partners are sometimes changed (1964, 270). Brueggemann proposes that in the divine-human conversation sometimes "both parties are transformed" (76). He introduces this idea in a discussion of rage and alienation which bring the divine-human conversation to a halt. Those who had been partners now become adversaries, distanced from one another. The resumption of discourse necessitates a change in both partners. Brueggemann writes first about humans and then about God:

> The conversation impinges upon those who are alienated and enraged, to transform them into creatures of praise. The conversation also impinges upon the silent, absent sovereign and draws God back into the pain and hope of the world. The conversation transforms both parties, permitting communion. (76)

For Brueggemann, the divine-human conversation holds the possibility of mutual transformation.

The what of conversational preaching—as interpretations, proposals, and wagers in need of the interpretations, proposals, and wagers of others—goes hand in hand with this redescription of revelation as a two-directional conversation that is always historically conditioned and that sometimes involves mutual transformation. In this two-way conversation, human self-disclosure is always partial because of the limited nature of human knowledge, particularly self-knowledge. L.-M. Dewailly's redescription of the Word of God suggests that divine self-disclosure is also partial.

Dewailly describes the Word as "the mystery which is [God's] divine reality" (1964, 290) and as "the secret of God" (289) told for all eternity to God's self (290). Thus the Word is "incommunicable" (289) to humans because the fullness of God's reality cannot adequately be expressed without God's "losing that which is properly divine in [the] Godhead" (290). What the Word reveals is partial and limited (293, 294) because "it is impossible to express worthily or even to conceive clearly and exactly what God is" (295). God "is only to be seen in [God's] silence" (295).

The Word of God is also Christ, who, Dewailly claims, "knows all but cannot say all" (293). Even in Christ's revelation of "what God has done, does, and will do," "the Word remains hidden" (293) because it is finally God's secret:

> The Word comes out of the mysterious silence of God but . . . cannot come out of it entirely. The Word remains enveloped in that silence and impregnated with it. The Word is the too weighty, too pregnant, incomprehensible fullness of God. (293)

In addition, the Word found in the writings of the biblical witnesses remains wrapped in mystery. If Christ "knows all but cannot say all," the apostles "do not say all because they do not know all" (293–94).

At the same time, the church must turn repeatedly to the Bible (295) for symbols and images that "are authentic expressions of divine reality under its different aspects," that "give us real holds on the secret without, however, any control over the absoluteness of this secret" (196). Dewailly further describes these biblical symbols and images:

> Their multiplicity suggests well the richness of [God's] reality by leaving a margin for the infinity of God. . . .
>
> The being of God, the unity, continuity, and the ultimate meaning of [God's] interventions among people—are always beyond the gate of our understanding, but by means of the word images of the Bible which are taken up and orchestrated in the liturgy, we can find them offered as nourishment for our contemplation. (296)

In the face of the Word's silence, faith always remains incomplete, awaiting that day when "we will see God face to face" (296). And that day, Dewailly claims, will be full of "immense surprises" (296).

The Word that Dewailly describes is not the purveyor of absolute truth or unequivocal knowledge of God. It is, rather, a silent, elusive Word that must be sought again and again in the multiplicity of biblical "word images" (ibid.). It is an incomprehensible Word this side of the eschaton with which we must engage in ongoing, relentless conversation.

Maureen P. Carroll (1983) likewise disassociates the Word form eternal truth or unchanging knowledge of God. Unlike Dewailly, who links the Word with the divine realm, however, Carroll links it with the human realm. Following Schillebeeckx, she identifies the Word as action that enhances human freedom. For her, the preached Word "puts a 'name' to the import of the *action* taken on behalf of the freedom of others" (45).

Although Dewailly and Carroll offer different redescriptions of the Word, both are compatible with conversational preaching. Dewailly's Word supports new understandings of revelation as ongoing divine-human conversation.

Carroll's Word suggests how the term *kerygma* can function in conversational preaching. In her discussions of the Word as inseparable from human freedom, the concept of freedom functions kerygmatically. What I mean is that Carroll has a clear concept of the heart or the core of the Word, that is, human freedom; her *kerygma,* although she never uses the word, is this concept of freedom. My proposal is that in conversational preaching the *kerygma* is no longer the unchanging core of the gospel, grounded in the apostles' preaching as once-and-for-all revelation. Instead, the *kerygma* might designate a temporary formulation of a slice of God's activity in the world that is critical for the contemporary church and that is grounded in revelation as an ongoing conversation with God, the Word, and biblical texts. The *kerygma* for one generation in one corner of the church might be human freedom; it will be different in a different generation in a different corner of the church. Given this redescription of the *kerygma,* a part of the work of preaching as a communal, ecclesial activity becomes formulating and reformulating the *kerygma*'s provisional content; that is, discerning those dimensions of the Word that become correctives for the future as the distortions of the past and present come into focus.

This understanding of the *kerygma* is implicit in Claude H. Thompson's re-thinking of C. H. Dodd (1962). For Thompson, understanding the *kerygma* involves looking not to the past or to propositional statements of fact but to the present and to believers' existential involvement with the *kerygma* as meaning (33). Thompson quotes Alfred North Whitehead: "Christ gave His life. It is for Christians to discern the doctrine."[11] Then Thompson claims, *"Christ inaugurated the kingdom. It is for Christians to clarify the meaning"* (25, Thompson's italics).

Thompson suggests that the *kerygma* does not consist of doctrines or meanings linked to objective realities or timeless truths that theologians and preachers formulate once and for all. Instead, doctrines and meanings must be discerned and clarified through existential involvement. Thompson suggests that the *kerygma* demands constant reinterpretation not only by preachers and theologians but also by "Christians" (25).

Revelation, Word, kerygma are all terms that, when redescribed, undergird conversational preaching's content as interpretations, proposals, and wagers. I am much less comfortable with the word *truth*. It is freighted for me with negative history, especially in homiletics. Too often in the past, "truth" as announced from the pulpit has excluded the experiences, interpretations, and convictions that have shaped my life and faith and the lives and faith of many others. My preference is to call a moratorium on the word *truth*. Such a moratorium would challenge preachers and homiletical scholars to confront how unconsciously, and sometimes ruthlessly, the word *truth* is used to designate partisan interpretations and personal wagers. In place of the word *truth* with its all-too-often assumed link to objective reality, I suggest we use the word *meaning* with its link to commitment and discipleship.

Domenico Grasso makes this shift from truth to meaning when he writes:

> We have here [in the writings of the early apostles] an account of events that really occurred: but what matters is not so much their truth as their meaning. Christ died and rose again for our salvation, that is, to give meaning to our lives by admitting us to participation in divine life, to the trinitarian dialogue, where human restlessness is stilled and life acquires meaning. Thus, in order to make known the true significance of all these facts, the Apostles had only one means: their life with Jesus, the contacts they had with Him for three years: eating and drinking with Him, listening to Him and seeing Him perform miracles. (1965, 169)

More important than truth is meaning and the testimony of life's experiences.

This shift to personal testimony is a key dimension of conversational preaching. Yet it poses a danger that Thielicke recognizes. He asks if preachers are limited to speaking only about the certainties in their own lives (1965, 52). "No," he answers and urges preachers to acknowledge that they are "helpless at certain points" because much "is still beyond" their experience and understanding (53).

Justo L. González and Catherine Gunsalus González combine redescriptions of revelation, Word, and truth in order to reinterpret preaching (1980). Their alternative, based on Latin American liberation theology, is "liberation preaching."[12]

Truth for González and González is neither a changeless universal, grounded in objective reality, nor an "is" (20), grounded in ontology. Instead, truth is grounded in history and eschatology. As "something that happens" (20), it opens human history toward God's future (20–21, 31), toward history's culmination in the fulfillment of God's promises for all humanity (60, 112).

Similarly, revelation is both historical and eschatological. It discloses God's activity within human history (20, 83–84) and invites human participation in history's movement toward its culmination in a new social order (22–24).

And finally for González and González, the Word also acquires new meanings. It is "God's word," spelled with a small "w." Severed from the church's traditional interpretation of Scripture and Christian doctrine (see 15, 16, 29–30), this "word" of God is best understood by the powerless (19), "the Simon Peters of today's world—the fisherfolk on a lake in Nicaragua, the political prisoners in South Africa, the women whose rights are trampled" (76). The world of this "word" is not the realm of "immutable essences, [or] eternal laws" (83), but history and history's end. Like truth and revelation, the "word" is "the record of God's action in history," or "God active in history" (83), announcing a new order as history's culmination (24, 112). The Bible ceases to be a mine for universal truths, kerygmatic formulas, or encoded intentionalities and becomes instead the source of *what we believe to be God's word* in the text for our concrete situation and struggle" (46, my italics). "What we believe to be God's word" is a wager and an interpretation inseparable from particular historical contexts and eschatological hope.

Are words like *revelation, Word, kerygma,* and *truth* still useful in discussions of preaching's content? I believe they are, if they are used self-critically and if their content is provisional and negotiable.

This discussion of the content of preaching pushes to the forefront a third, ineluctable question. Conversational preaching claims that preaching's content—severed from absolute claims about revelation, Word, *kerygma,* and truth—consists of tentative partisan interpretations, proposals that invite additional proposals, and personal wagers aware of other wagers. Are then all interpretations, proposals, and wagers acceptable?

In recent years, as threats to certainty have crept into the conversations at the homiletical table, the issue of safeguards that can guarantee the faithfulness of preaching's content has surfaced time and again. Many safeguards have been proposed.

Roman Catholic scholars tend to emphasize some aspect of the church. Schmaus claims that the doctrine of infallibility guards revelation from error and, by extension, preaching (1966, 128–29). Grasso's argument is more complex. Linking preaching and personal testimony, he asks, "Is it not possible that the witness be a swindler who wants to deceive us?" (1965, 170). His answer is "No." If preachers deceive, they must first deceive themselves, because they witness to that which they have experienced and to which they are dedicated. A second question then arises, What prevents self-deception? Grasso's answer is "collective testimony"[13]:

> While it is possible that one individual may be deceived, or even a certain number of individuals, it becomes less and less probable when millions accept the message and live by it, especially when accepting the message means sacrifice and renunciation. (171–72)

The locating of that which safeguards preaching's content in the church is characteristic of Roman Catholic scholarship.

Ritschl (1960) expresses the conviction of many Protestant scholars. He urges the church to "test the word of the sermon by going back to [the] written witness" of the Word of God (144). Thus the faithfulness of preaching's content is tied to Scripture. Since Scripture must be interpreted, however, the critical question becomes, "Where does the control over the interpretive process lie?" (Long 1989a, 26). Long answers, and many Protestant scholars agree, that "the text" (26) holds the clues for its own interpretation.

If, however, every interpretation of every text is freighted with the biases of the interpreters, then the text alone is not an adequate safeguard. Some Protestant scholars pair Scripture with a second safeguard—for example, serious engagement with the text plus the leading of the Spirit (Beardslee and others 1989, 49) or the Bible and the congregation. Henry Mitchell claims that "the contemporary Christian audience knows when the imaginative details [of a sermon] stray wide of the Bible truth and goal" (1977, 156).

A more fundamental question for me becomes, *Who* exercises control over the interpretive process and therefore over preaching's content? Is the answer the preacher, the clergy, and the scholars? Or is the answer all the partners in the church's central conversations? Those who exercise control over preaching's content are, in fact, all those who are invited to participate in the formative conversations of the people of God. My conviction is that control over preaching's content belongs to all the various partners in the multiple conversations preaching fosters.

For me, the critical issue in conversational preaching is not whether preaching meets some absolute standard of orthodoxy but whether sermonic interpretations, proposals, and wagers serve to foster all the central conversations of the church as the people of God, whether they upbuild the communities of faith in their local and global configurations (see 1 Cor. 14:12), and whether they respect and invite the voices of the silenced, the disenfranchised, the poor, and women.

Preaching's content will shift and shuffle until the eschaton. *Kerygmas* will rise and fall, only to rise and fall again. An interpretation of Scripture that is essential for one generation in one location will give way to a different interpretation in the next generation. The hope that preaching's content will remain faithful lies in the grace of God and the vitality of all the multiple ecclesial conversations.

Summary

What is the content of preaching in conversational preaching? It is a tentative interpretation of a biblical text and of God's activity in the world as meaning that makes life bearable and worthwhile (Browne 1958, 34). It is a proposal that creates space for genuine conversation, invites counterproposals, and fosters mutual encouragement, edification, and sometimes transformation among all the participants in the church's central conversations. It is a wager on the part of the preacher, a genuine yet humble confession of faith that acknowledges its particularity and self-interest and seeks the corrective and confirmation of others' wagers.

This proposal for a redescription of preaching's content entails redescriptions of such words as *revelation, Word, kerygma,* and *truth.* Revelation becomes an ongoing, two-directional divine-human conversation. The Word of God becomes that which reveals and yet conceals, participating in both divine mystery and the particularity of human experience. The *kerygma* is a provisional formulation of a portion of the gospel for a particular generation in a particular location. Truth, always fragmentary and ambiguous, awaits disclosure in the eschaton. More important than truth are meaning and testimony. An important conviction of conversational preaching is that, until the eschaton, the content of words like *revelation, Word, kerygma, truth, meaning,* and *testimony* remains tentative, incomplete, particular, and negotiable.

Another important conviction in this redescription of preaching's content is that discerning this provisional content of preaching belongs to the entire people of God. Conversational preaching grows out of and flows into the life-giving conversations that by God's grace are ever-broadening to include a multiplicity of experiences, interpretations of texts, and construals of the gospel.

How then do we test preaching's content? We do it as we participate daily, weekly, over a lifetime in the life-giving conversations that form and reform the people of God.

Rethinking Sermonic Language

These whys and whats of conversational preaching entail new probes into the hows of preaching. And asking how one preaches a conversational sermon invites a rethinking of sermonic language, based on the conviction that language always unavoidably reflects the limitations and sinful distortions of its users.

Two characteristics of sermonic language come to the forefront in conversational preaching. First, sermonic language is confessional, reflecting the accumulated and ongoing experiences of the people of God. And second, in conversational preaching sermonic language is evocative, able to generate multiple meanings.

Three homiletical scholars discuss the confessional dimension of sermonic language. Thor Hall argues that the language of faith is always the language of confession (1971):

> Theological statements are neither "indicative" (having reference to the empirical world) nor "analytical" (consisting in relating various definitions to one another); they are "convictional." As such they do have reference to "reality," though all that needs to be said about the reality to which they refer is that it is "real" for those who speak this way.[14]

What is important about theological discourse, Hall claims, "is the fact that this sort of language involves the user—the *homo loguens*—totally" (86). In theological discourse, speakers become "part of the language, the conviction" (86). These speakers belong to religious communities that understand the universe through a normative myth, story, image, or set of concepts that they believe to be a true reflection and explanation of reality (86–87). Theological language, therefore, expresses more the convictions of religious communities than the actuality of God. Hall explains, to think that theological language expresses the "nature," the "being," or the "essence" of God "would be a presumptuous denial both of the limits of human understanding and of the infinite transcendence and 'otherness' of God" (90). The language of faith is always "confessional," representing convictions to which believers have come through their experiences and through the influence of those who have believed before them (90).

Sittler addresses the confessional nature of the language of faith as a theological issue. He contends that theology has been severed from former philosophical, moral, and existential alliances and is therefore thrown back on its own resources (1966, 62). These resources include "the terms, episodes, [and] patterns of the biblical story" (62) as well as the primary resource, "the organic historical fact-world of a community affirming itself to be a community by the word of God" (63). Thus Sittler suggests that the language of faith is confessional because, like theology, its references are the biblical story and the community of faith.

Hall and Sittler imply that as preachers and worshipers we say in effect, "We *believe* that the language of faith somehow reflects, albeit imperfectly, humanity's relationship to God and the eschatological reality that God is bringing into being. Until the eschaton, however, we see in a mirror dimly and know only in part (1 Cor. 13:12). Until the eschaton, we live by faith and hope, not by sight (Heb. 11:1, Rom. 8:24–25)." Such believing is sustainable only within the community of faith, where we test our beliefs and practices by the biblical witnesses and trust that there is an ongoing Word from God.

For Hall and Sittler, the language of faith *is* confessional. For Thielicke, the language of faith *should be* confessional in that it should reflect the preacher's personal convictions (1965). Thielicke describes two linguistic problems that plague the preacher. Narrowly, the language of faith is always in danger of being impure, "freighted with a history" so that its original meaning is altered (36). Broadly, all contemporary language is "untrue" (45). At one time language was "true" in that it "grasped reality," but now it is "empty of all content" (45).[15] Thielicke solves both these problems by claiming that the language of preaching must reflect the preacher's lived faith (4–11). Words like *grace, sin,* and *Christ* require interpretation (37) and should not be passed on "undigested" (40). Rather, the vocabulary of the church must have "passed through" and transformed the preacher into a "witness" (47, see 50). Thielicke does not break the link between "Christian words" (36) and truth. These words are not lies but the "vehicles of a sunken truth" (47). At the same time, the primary focus shifts from truth as an external reality to truth as an experience (50) and a confession (47) on the part of the preacher as "witness" (47).[16]

One characteristic of sermonic language in conversational preaching is its confessional quality. In addition to its being inevitably confessional, the language preachers choose should have so shaped their lives that it expresses the convictions out of which and into which they are living.

A second characteristic of sermonic language is its multivalence. Bernard Brandon Scott discusses the fact that all language *is* evocative of multiple meanings; Fred B. Craddock discusses the fact that sermonic language *should be* evocative.

Scott's claim is that language in general possesses a surplus of meaning (1985, 75) and thus inevitably generates multiple meanings. Scott explains that a word consists of both a Pointer, which is its physical sound or combination of letters, and an Idea, which is its mental image[17]:

> When we look up a Word that we do not understand, we are seeking to form an Idea for the Pointer we find on the page. Because we cannot combine Pointer with Idea, we cannot form a Word. What the dictionary provides in its definition is the association of the Idea with other related Ideas. We associate these known Ideas to create a new Idea for our Pointer. (20).

The problem with language is that the relationship between a Pointer and an Idea is never fixed (29). The Idea to which a word points is arbitrary, unstable, and ever-changing. At the very heart of language is "a basic instability and changeability" (29). Meaning then does not reside in a stable relationship between a Pointer and an Idea. Rather, "meaning cannot be divorced from human beings who understand" (14); it is "relational" and demands "imaginative interaction" (17, see 45). Inevitably, "our individual perspectives" influence the meanings of words (14, see 72). Because of this inherent instability, words inevitably generate a variety of meanings (45). Particularly, a poetic sentence, like "The Word became flesh and pitched its tent among us" (25–26), "is suggestive of meaning(s). It has no single, simple meaning. It asks the reader to play imaginatively with its possibilities" (27).

Craddock's hope is that sermonic language will intentionally activate meanings within the congregation (1974). He wants preachers "to engage the hearer[s] in the pursuit of an issue or an idea so that [they] will think [their] own thoughts and experience [their] own feelings in the presence of Christ and in the light of the Gospel" (157). Craddock therefore suggests that words be "set in silence, during which time the hearers speak" (95). He advocates "images which awaken images" (95). He calls for "the use of few words suggesting the main lines of a picture" (93) so that the worshipers who "fill in the details and complete the image" arrive "at new meaning and insight" (93). Craddock urges preachers to choose words that are deliberately evocative and suggestive.

Sermonic language that is confessional and evocative spotlights the community of faith as opposed to the preacher. Traditional views of preaching emphasize the power of sermonic language to persuade. Conversational preaching is wary of the persuasive character of language: Will preachers present as normative or universal that which is particular and individual? Kerygmatic views of preaching assume the power of sermonic language so to represent the *kerygma* that the congregation participates in a saving event. Conversational preaching is wary of the representational character of language: Will preachers ignore the biases inherent in every formulation of the *kerygma?* Transformational views of preaching build on the power of sermonic language to "do" or "perform" a text, to create a new reality, or to transform values, worldviews, or ways of being in the world. Conversational preaching is wary of the performative dimension of language: Will preachers who seek to perform texts, create new realities, or transform the worshipers be honest that their presentations of texts, new realities, and gospel values, worldviews, or ways of being in the world are constructs reflecting their own biases? In conversational preaching, confessional language belongs to the community of faith, and evocative language invites those gathered to participate in the community's ongoing, central conversations.

Summary

How does one preach a conversational sermon? In part, by using language that is confessional and generative of multiple meanings.

Sermonic language is inevitably confessional as it expresses and constructs the life experiences of faith communities.[18] Sermonic language can also be intentionally confessional, as preachers articulate their own wagers and the wagers of others and as communities appropriate and rethink the language of the Bible, ecclesial traditions, and the global church.

In addition, sermonic language inevitably generates a variety of meanings. Embracing the evocative dimension of words, preachers can intentionally invite the worshipers to formulate their own meanings beside, ahead of, and over against the sermon's meanings. Preachers can choose words that evoke a variety of life experiences, interpretations, and convictions.

How does one preach a conversational sermon? In part by choosing words, old and new, that both describe the contours of what is known and probe the mysteries of what is elusive; by choosing words, old and new, that open up the richness and the depths of life's myriad experiences and faith's hidden treasures.

How does one preach a conversational sermon? In part, by realizing that although *one* may do the speaking, the preacher is never isolated or alone. The one speaks the language of the community of faith in its historical and global configurations. The one speaks with, among, and sometimes on behalf of others because she or he has already in countless prior conversations been speaking with, among, and sometimes on behalf of others. The one speaks of personal experiences, interpretative possibilities, and convictions, using words that invite the personal experiences, interpretations, and convictions of all the worshipers as participants in the ongoing, communal conversations.

Preaching a conversational sermon is in part a matter of sermonic language that is confessional and evocative.

Rethinking
Sermonic Form

The hows of preaching include sermonic form as well as sermonic language. Asking how one preaches a conversational sermon is also an invitation to revisit the issue of sermonic form.

Form, like language, is never objective or innocent. Since no single form can ever grasp the whole of human experience, every form represents or imposes an order on a limited segment of experience. Thus, whether representing or imposing order, a form reflects the limitations of those who use it and is a strategy in service of partisan convictions.[19]

In traditional views of preaching, sermonic forms seek to transmit objective truth via the sermon's message or central idea. In kerygmatic views of preaching, sermonic forms seek to communicate the *kerygma* as both knowledge about God and God's saving activity. In transformational views of preaching, sermonic forms seek to convey an experience that transforms the congregation's values, attitudes, ways of being in the world, or worldviews. In conversational views of preaching, sermonic forms seek to engage the community of faith in its central, ongoing conversations.

Before turning to specific forms that foster conversational preaching, I want to highlight three shifts in emphasis that undergird my discussion of sermonic form. Each shift in emphasis raises a question about the forms of preaching.

The first shift is from a focus on the effect of the individual sermon to an interest in the cumulative effects of preaching. Kerygmatic and transformational scholars who emphasize the individual sermon as a saving or transforming event seldom discuss preaching's cumulative effect. Such discussions are characteristic, however, of traditional preaching where preaching is linked with teaching. One traditional scholar likens preaching to eating "nicely prepared meal[s]" over many years (Ireson 1958, 26). The question that arises for conversational preaching is, What forms of preaching, other than those that emphasize instruction, take seriously the cumulative nature of preaching?

The second shift in emphasis of conversational preaching is to an explicit recognition of preaching as open discourse that invites believers to search for meaning. John Brokhoff discusses the distinction between open and closed discourse (1985). An address, he claims, is open discourse. It "leaves room for questions and discussion" (27); it participates in the ongoing search for truth (28). A sermon, however, is closed discourse. It expresses known truth: "In a sermon God speaks a final word on matters of faith and life" (28).

Conversational preaching considers a sermon to be open discourse. A number of homiletical scholars agree. William Muehl writes that "the biblical faith is finally complex because the God to whom it bears witness is veiled in mystery. . . . It is, therefore, the first responsibility of preaching to engage men and women in a search which is the very essence of human existence in history" (1986, 27). William K. McElvaney also calls for a preaching style that involves a "mutual search" instead of "dogmatic coercion" (1989, 65). He suggests that preaching's style be "confessional, vulnerable," and "inquiring" (64–66). Such preaching "is conducive to growth for both preacher and listener" (66) and is characterized by a "confessional posture" in which preachers are not afraid to reveal their faith struggles (66). Some preaching then is about a search in which the preacher and the congregation are partners. Sheldon A. Tostengard focuses this search into a question (1989). He proposes with Greek Testament scholar Ernst Käsemann that the critical question for the church today is, "What does it mean for the church, and for me, to be a disciple of Jesus just now?" (17). The question that this emphasis raises for conversational preaching is, What sermonic forms encourage the communal search for meaning, for provisional answers to the question about contemporary discipleship?

The third shift in emphasis that characterizes conversational preaching involves the perception of what art is all about and what artists are doing in their art. Gene E. Bartlett reflects one understanding of art (1962). The artist and the writer "can perceive the essential meaning of an area of beauty, put it into an art form, and impart it to others" (18). Here his understanding of art correlates with how some advocates of traditional and kerygmatic preaching view the tasks of sermon making. Like artists, preachers first discern meaning or truth; then they choose a form through which to communicate this meaning or truth. Bartlett also describes preaching as "an art by which we find the form that releases the experience to those who hear" (58). Here his kerygmatic views of preaching begin to overlap with transformational views. For Bartlett, the sermon, like art, seeks to convey or facilitate a particular meaning or experience. Art thus expresses an idea already discovered or "releases" (58) in others an experience already experienced.

Conversational preaching understands art differently, along with a few homiletical scholars. Describing the point of view of the artist, John Killinger claims that artists discover something as they paint or compose poems (1969, 23). Eugene L. Lowry similarly points to novelists who claim that they do not always know where their story is going before they start writing (1985, 16, 49). Scott writes, "Actually an author discovers meaning in the process of writing" (1985, 16). Meaning, in this understanding of art, is not something the artist discovers first and then seeks to impart through an artistic medium. Rather, art is a process through which the artist searches for meaning.[20]

Walter J. Burghardt expresses essentially the same understanding of art from a different point of view—that of the reader (1983). Following Hans-Georg Gadamer, Burghardt claims that for the reader the meaning of a classical text is inexhaustible (30). Meaning exceeds the conscious intention of the author so that reading involves the reader in the formulation of meaning. For readers, then, classical texts involve them in a search for meaning. Lowry similarly claims that narratives generate meaning.[21] And Scott claims that "real poetry" (1985, 25) "is suggestive of meaning(s)" (27). For the reader, as well as for the artist, some art involves discovering meaning that is not fixed or predetermined.

Some art is not a strategy whereby the artist seeks to impart preconceived meaning or truth to others. Some art seeks to reflect the experience of discovery on the part of the artist and to invite the readers or viewers to become interpreters of meaning. Meaning, divorced from a fixed message, becomes multilayered and open. And the process of creating and interpreting becomes heuristic, yielding unexpected discoveries. The question for conversational preaching is, What forms of preaching can both reflect the experience of discovery on the part of the preacher and engage the worshipers as interpreters who are responsible for discovering their own meanings?

Three questions preface this discussion of sermonic forms: (1) What forms of preaching, other than those that aim to instruct, take seriously the cumulative nature of preaching? (2) What sermonic forms encourage the communal search for meaning, particularly in terms of contemporary discipleship? And (3) What forms of preaching are heuristic both for the preacher and the congregation?

The two forms that I will describe are, first, a combination of inductive and narrative, and, second, story. My discussion of these two forms is intended to be suggestive, not exhaustive.[22] Any sermon form that offers tentative interpretations, proposals, or wagers can serve conversational preaching.

The first form charts the preacher's journey toward the discovery of meaning and invites others to "think [their] own thoughts and experience [their] own feelings" (Craddock 1974, 157) as they formulate their own meanings. My proposal here builds on the insights of H. Grady Davis, Craddock, and Lowry.

Davis describes a form that he labels "a question propounded" (1958, 154–57). A sermon that takes this shape represents a genuine search on the part of the preacher for answers. The preacher's goal, however, is not to hand over a previously conceived answer. Examining a sermon by Arthur Gossip, Davis concludes that the question "remains a question to be answered by" the worshipers (156) and the sermon "gives one man's [Gossip's] answer, his witness that the gospel has answered the question for him" (156–57).

Davis's "question propounded" is similar to the inductive form that Craddock popularized (1974). Both forms reflect a quest, or a search, on the part of the preacher; both invite the worshipers to embark on their own parallel, even divergent, journeys. Davis's form is generated by a question; Craddock's inductive form is generated by a text and the preacher's inductive arrival at meaning. Craddock's preacher invites the congregation to retrace a journey the preacher has already taken toward an understanding of the text (see 125, 57). Craddock's inductive sermon aims to reflect some of "the thrill of potential discovery" that characterizes exegesis (124).

According to Craddock, the inductive preacher is continually looking in two directions. One is toward the specific particulars of human experience (57, 58, 61). By paying attention to life's particulars, the preacher hopes "to activate" in the congregation meanings that correlate with what the sermon is about (60). The other direction is toward the preacher's own journey of finding meaning in the text, a journey that influences the sermon's movement.

Craddock's inductive sermon form fosters conversational preaching when the sermon genuinely searches for meaning at the intersection between a biblical text and the lives of the preacher and worshipers, or between faith and life experiences. It also fosters conversational preaching when the preacher understands that the sermon offers *a proposal* about the text's meaning—not *the* point, encoded experience, or proper performance of the text. Craddock's inductive form seeks to invite the congregation to formulate their own meanings, reflect on their own experiences, confirm or reconfigure their faith commitments, or create their own performances of the text in response to the sermon.

Lowry's narrative sermon form consists of a plot that moves from tension to resolution (1980, 1985, 1989, 1990). It too fosters conversational preaching by inviting the congregation to reflect on their own faith and experiences and arrive at their own conclusions. From the point of view of the preacher, the narrative sermon begins by articulating a tension, ambiguity, or disequilibrium that is felt by the preacher and, it is hoped, the congregation. The sermon then directly or indirectly reflects the preacher's journey toward resolution as that journey has been broadened by an awareness of a variety of experiences within the congregation, the church, and the world. From the point of view of the worshipers, the narrative sermon is an opportunity for them to become interpreters: like the inductive sermon, it invites them to follow the guidance of the Holy Spirit, to join the conversation with the biblical text, and to reconfigure or confirm the sermon's interpretations, proposals, and wagers. The sermon's end is not the worshipers' arrival at the preacher's proposed resolution but their arrival at their own provisional resolutions or resting-places on the journey. The sermon's end is a proper ending to the sermon's particular plot.[23]

Lowry's narrative form is both like and unlike Craddock's inductive form. Like Craddock, Lowry proposes a form that charts a process of discovery. Unlike Craddock's preacher, however, Lowry's preacher sometimes begins shaping the sermon by clarifying the opening tension long before the sermon's end is evident. This starting at the beginning warrants additional attention. Having identified the trouble, the narrative preacher must then wait for the tension or ambiguity to work itself toward some form of resolution, resting-place, or proper ending. Lowry's understanding of narrative sermon form borrows from Davis's "generative idea" (1958) the conviction that the full-grown sermon is hidden in the seed. For Davis, the seed is the generative idea.[24] Lowry, in *The Homiletical Plot* (1980), draws heavily on Davis's "generative idea." But in his later books, he moves beyond Davis's focus on an idea and suggests that the end of the plot is hidden in its beginning. For Lowry, the seed is the tension, ambiguity, or disequilibrium that sets the sermon's plot on its way. Narrative form, then, is a design that is not consciously crafted. Rather, it is the flowering of the sermonic seed that takes root and grows within the preacher.

Lowry thus offers a sermon form that does not depend on the preacher's having a preconceived message, a sermonic idea, or a statement of focus. Challenging the notion that the preacher should state the meaning of every sermon in one simple sentence, Browne asks, "To what one unambiguous sentence could a Christmas sermon be reduced?" (1958, 28). He continues, "If all that a sermon or a poem said could be put in one sentence, would there be any point in making sermons or poems?" (28). Lowry suggests a form by which a sermon can have unity and coherence without its having a central idea or focal sentence. The plot gives unity and coherence to the narrative sermon as it does to a novel or short story.[25] Such a sermon does not necessarily result in the worshipers' consent to a preconceived message, nor in their experiencing a particular event. Rather, the sermon potentially gives rise to a variety of experiences and interpretations.

Both inductive and narrative sermon forms are strategies that by recharting the preacher's discovery of meaning invite the worshipers to discover their

own meanings.[26] The preacher might choose in a sermon to rechart the journey that resulted in personal transformation, but the sermon's aim is not for
the congregation to experience the same transformation. Rather, conversational preachers acknowledge, to the extent that they are able, the particularity of their experiences and convictions and seek to reflect in their sermons a
variety of experiences and convictions that may not be their own but are represented in the congregation, the larger household of God, and the world.

A second sermonic form that fosters conversational preaching is a type of
story preaching that allows the story to generate its own meanings. No moral
or explanation, explicit or implicit, accompanies this story-sermon. Richard
Thulin values story-sermons because they give the congregation "freedom to
create their own meanings" (1990, 12). Story preaching thus has the potential
to engage the congregation in shaping meanings that far exceed the set of
meanings the sermon created in the preacher's own life.[27] Again, one version
starts at the end and another version starts at the beginning.

The inductive version of story preaching begins with the end of the story.
Richard A. Jensen gives the following advice:

> In order to create a story the first thing we must do is to have a fairly clear
> idea of what we want the story to accomplish. With that idea in place we
> can proceed to outline the potential story (an outline which may experience
> much change during the actual process of writing) sketching out the setting
> of the story, the chief characters, the problem (plot) that will need resolu-
> tion, the episodes of the story itself and the conclusion toward which we are
> striving. (1980, 149)

Although the preacher knows the conclusion, Jensen insists that the story-sermon should be open-ended. The preacher need not end by saying, "The point
of this story is . . ." (145). Rather, the preacher's personal meaning should never
be imposed on the congregation, limiting the story to one meaning or application. Jensen claims that in story preaching "we give up final control over the
content of what we preach. We cannot know how the people sitting in [the]
pews will complete our story and apply it to their own life. Story preaching,
therefore, is a faith venture. The preacher dares to believe that the Spirit of
God may move even where he or she has given up control. Risky indeed!"
(147). All preaching to some extent shares this risk.[28] Jensen claims, "We fool
ourselves if we think everyone gets the point of didactic or even proclamatory
preaching" (145). For this reason, in traditional and kerygmatic theories a story-
sermon is deliberately crafted to be clear in order to get its point across, like
an Aesop fable. In conversational preaching, however, the story-sermon is deliberately crafted to invite the worshipers into the sermonic process as interpreters of the story's meaning.

A second version of story preaching is narrative, shaped by a plot that begins at the beginning. The story begins with disequilibrium. After the disequi-

librium has been adequately explored and expanded beyond the preacher's own personal experience, the story-sermon moves toward new, provisional equilibrium.

These two versions of story preaching do not directly or indirectly illustrate a truth or revolve around a single focus. On the contrary, in conversational preaching they purposefully invite a variety of meanings and revolve around a single but multileveled move from beginning to end, from tension to temporary resting-place. Frank J. McNulty, after seeing an Arthur Miller play, observed that the playwright "said some significant things about life. . . . And he did more, because his play set off in me a whole series of reflections about the complex nature of the redemptive process" (1985, 7). Like a provocative play, a story-sermon has the potential to "set off" in the congregation "a whole series of reflections" (ibid.). These reflections are not ends in themselves but constitute essential components of the larger conversations that are central in each congregation and the larger communities of faith.

Summary

Two forms of preaching that serve conversational preaching are a recharting of the preacher's journey toward meaning and story. Both reflect new emphases in conversational preaching.

They value the cumulative nature of preaching because they seek to nurture the church as a community of interpreters who value their own experiences and faith commitments, wrestle with the Holy Spirit and texts, and make their own decisions. Such a discerning, mutually edifying, self-critical community of interpreters is not shaped or sustained by a single sermon but by countless sermons week after week, year after year.

These two forms also encourage the search for communal meanings as the preacher and the congregation go "explor[ing] together in wonder, humility, and gratitude" (Craddock 1974, 64). These two forms allow the preacher and the congregation to join together in an ongoing search for provisional answers to such critical questions as "What does it mean for the church, and for me, to be a disciple of Jesus just now?" (Tostengard 1989, 17).

Finally, both forms of preaching are heuristic for the preacher and the congregation. They reflect and invite discoveries that confirm and reconfigure meanings, identities, wagers, values, ways of being in the world, and ecclesial agendas. Thus they represent "serious attempts to develop a different, more ecclesial rather than clerical style of preaching" (Schüssler Fiorenza 1983, 49).

A significant consequence of these forms is that the conversational preacher relinquishes control of the sermon's reception. The success of the sermon is not contingent on the worshipers' accurately receiving a preconceived message or experiencing a carefully orchestrated event. Instead, conversational forms acknowledge that the sermon's meanings lie in the interaction between the Spirit and the congregation as a community of interpreters.

A New Voice
at the Homiletical Table

On one level my proposal is a compilation of voices already present in the margins of the homiletical literature. Together these marginal voices crowding around the table constitute an alternative voice in the homiletical conversation. On another level, my proposal represents my reflections on my own experiences of being in the pulpit and the pew. This is my tentative conclusion, my temporary resting-place on a much longer personal journey. On still another level, my proposal is an effort to articulate an understanding of preaching that resonates with the convictions, experiences, and hopes of others. I dare to hope that there are others who hold similar beliefs about what we are doing when we rise to preach and what we hope for when we sit in the pew while others preach.

Joining the conversation around the homiletical table, this proposal now seeks the correction, the confirmation, the enlargement, the challenge of the multitude of other voices both within and outside the homiletical conversation.

Silence. She Is Six Years Old*

Lynn Emanuel

She sleeps on a cot in the living room.
This is her father's mother's house.
And in the kitchen the men run their knife blades
across the oilcloth with roses on the table
and grandmother cooks them steak and eggs.
She is pretending to be asleep but she is listening
to the men talking about their friends
and grandmother in her white dress
walks back and forth past the door
and a hand reaches for salt and water.
Her father talks about divorce.
Now it is quiet.
Grandmother has left, her tight stockings
showed rainbows
and someone's upstairs undressing,
his dog tags making faint noise.
Her father walks into the room.
He is naked and there are certain
parts of him that are shadows.
And he pulls the blankets to the floor
and then the sheet—as if not to wake her—
and he lifts her up and whispers his wife's name—
Rachel, Rachel
and he takes her hand, small with its clean nails,
and he puts it to the dark:

Oh Rae, Oh Rachel he says
and over his shoulder she can see
the long hall mirror framed in black wood
and she smells lavender in her father's hair
when he gets up, first only his hands
and knees like someone playing horse,
and puts her on the chair
and she sits and rocks like a deaf woman.

*Repeatedly throughout the following chapter and in chapter 4, I refer to the silenced, or occasionally the muted or abused. These selections depict real people: Maria, whose mother, throughout Maria's childhood, burned her genitals with cigarettes; Claudine, who was molested at age 4 by a kindergarten worker, and Rachel's daughter whose story is told above. The silenced also include boys and men. Too often the silenced remain silent because their stories—so full of pain and horror—are hard to tell *and hard to hear*. Yet the community of faith is impoverished and I believe unfaithful when it cannot invite these stores into its central conversations and embrace the tellers of the stories. This selection is included as a reminder, particularly to myself, that I must not retreat from the most vulnerable who belong at the homiletical round table.

5 ☙ The Conversation Broadens

So far I have been listening exclusively to voices at the homiletical table, dominant and marginal voices present in the homiletical literature. Turning from this conversation, I wonder: If the theoretical aspects of conversational preaching described in chapter 4 relate to actual preaching practices, what more can be said about conversational preaching by those outside the field of homiletics? What insights from other disciplines can help our reflecting, describing, and naming? In this chapter I turn for clues to writers whose primary focus is not preaching.

While conversational preaching seeks to gather up and name existing practices, it is not a technique or method that can be added to other techniques and methods. It is at heart a connected way of being that issues in connected ways of speaking. At this point I do not know exactly its how-tos; I only recognize, or think I recognize, its broad brushstrokes and basic convictions.

In this chapter I will revisit and augment, based on forays outside the field of homiletics, five characteristics that seem to me at the heart of conversational preaching: it is communal, nonhierarchical, personal, inclusive, and scriptural. As in chapter 4, my suggestions and descriptions are meant to be preliminary, not exhaustive. I appeal to those who resonate with my proposal to make their own suggestions and descriptions as we seek to probe and name this practice I have called, provisionally, "conversational preaching."

The Ecclesial Community

First, conversational preaching is communal, growing out of the community ethos of those gathered for worship and nurturing a larger sense of connectedness.

The context for conversational preaching within the homiletical literature is the priesthood of all believers. Outside the field of homiletics, other images describe the sense of ecclesial community that is the matrix for conversational preaching. These images include "a discipleship of equals" and "a community of friends."[1] Conversational preaching emerges among believers who seek to be "a household where everyone gathers around the common table to break bread and to share table talk and hospitality" (Russell 1993, 42).

Puerto Rican veterinarian-turned-New-York-City-pastor, Loida Martell Otero images the church as *familia*.[2] Within the Hispanic culture, she explains, "the family unit is very important" (1994, 79). The Hispanic Protestant church "is the coming together of brothers and sisters in Christ. The parallel concept in the Hebrew Bible is the *mishpahah,* the clan, tribe or extended family. The Church becomes a "community family," where young and old, rich or poor, single, divorced or married, all are welcomed, nurtured, cared for, and treated as children of God" (79). This sense of belonging to an ecclesial family is a reality within the Hispanic Protestant church. The church "is the place where we feel comfortable to speak out with our hearts and to share our thoughts" (80). In the church, "we feel safe to share among those who we know will not ridicule us or dismiss us. We feel comfortable enough to question and be questioned, as we seek to discern God's will and speaking in our lives" (82).

Conversational preaching is communal, presupposing a sense of trust and safety that allows all "to speak out with our hearts and to share our thoughts" (ibid.). Outside such a communal ethos, in a hostile environment where the preacher feels embattled or isolated, I do not believe that conversational preaching can be sustained. It is inextricable from a sense of connectedness between the preacher and the worshipers and among worshipers who all share membership in the household of God as sisters and brothers in Christ.

Precisely because of this strong sense of connectedness within the community of faith, conversational preaching emphasizes the importance of sustained conversation with other communities of faith and with those on the margins—the broken, the silenced, the shunned. The gathered community is not an isolated enclave of "birds of a feather." Rather, connectedness within the congregation is inseparable from connectedness beyond the congregation. Theologian Letty M. Russell sets the local faith community in conversation with other "communities of faith and struggle" (1993, 36) for the purpose of "mutual judgment and correction of Christian performance" (94). In addition, she claims, the community is primarily connected "to Christ" (18) as the host (12) who is "found with the outsiders" (197, see 43); through Christ, therefore, it is connected to the oppressed, "those on the periphery of church and society" (134, see 18, 43). The community of faith is a local circle of friends that seeks "to make connections across dividing lines of religion, culture, race, class, gender, and sexual orientation so that the church and world become connected as a circle of friends" (19).

Outside the literature of homiletics, conversational preaching's communal character is augmented by those who describe the community of faith both internally and externally from the perspective of connectedness and solidarity.

The Absence of Hierarchy

The second characteristic of conversational preaching is that it is nonhierarchical.[3] Around the margins of the homiletical literature are hints of nonhierarchical understandings of power. Russell, however, redescribes power, authority, and leadership based on the practices of women pastors who "prefer not to be 'set apart' from their congregations, since they develop relationships among the people as those who share their baptism and commitment" (1993, 52). These women exercise their leadership by sharing power; theirs is a "shared authority in community" (57). Power is no longer "a zero sum game that requires competition and hoarding in order to 'win.' Rather, power and leadership gifts multiply as they are shared and more and more persons become partners in communities of faith and struggle. . . . Power is seen as something to be multiplied and shared rather than accumulated at the top" (56–57).

The goal of shared leadership is the building up of the church (55, 64, 66) so that all those who are baptized for ministry are equipped to fulfill their ministry (52). Thus all the members of the community become leaders, especially those on the margins who do not think they are "somebody" (57). Russell's redescriptions of authority, power, and leadership lead her to call for "a moratorium wherever possible on language reflecting distinctions between laity and clergy" (64).

Russell concedes that the particular shapes of shared leadership are still emerging (47, 72). I suggest that conversational preaching is one of these emergent forms of shared leadership. And if the details of these emergent forms of shared leadership are still unclear, the broad brushstrokes are recognizable: the new paradigm of nonhierarchical leadership "seeks to move away from the traditions of ordination and orders as authority of domination and to emphasize instead authority exercised in community" (73).

In such a nonhierarchal context, where power, leadership, and authority are shared, conversational preaching describes the whole of preaching as an ethos that surrounds the pulpit, traditionally a place of power. This nonhierarchical ethos perhaps leads those who are ordained to resist monopolizing the pulpit and to reenvision their role as ensuring that preaching occurs. This ethos perhaps leads the community of faith regularly to invite others, particularly laity, to preach. The term *preacher,* then, is not a synonym for one who is ordained or for the minister who controls access to the pulpit. Rather, it refers to the one whose function for the particular service of worship is to offer the sermon as one exchange in the ongoing conversations of the community.

This dimension of conversational preaching is linked to the communal dimension noted above. Nonhierarchical relationships begin to emerge among those who seek to be sisters and brothers in Christ. Within the household of God, domination and submission give way to partnership and cooperation; clericalism, or the hierarchical relationship between clergy and laity, disappears; everyone participates in setting the church's agenda and carrying out the church's ministry; and, in particular, those who are most marginal, whose voices have been excluded and silenced, are valued and invited back into the life-restoring conversations.

Personal Experience

A third characteristic of conversational preaching is its personal or autobiographical quality. At one level, conversational preaching is personal testimony, whether or not the preacher uses the personal pronoun "I" in the sermon. Here I revisit and augment the claims that conversational preaching's content is personal wagers and testimonies and its forms reflect the preacher's wrestling with a text.

Writer of children's stories Katherine Paterson (1981, 1989) offers four images for fiction writing that I appropriate for conversational preaching. Characteristic of each image is a personal or autobiographical dimension.

First, for Paterson, fiction writing begins with "a sound in the heart," an image drawn from one of the Japanese ideographs for *idea* (1989, 28, 45). She explains:

> In Japanese, the word is *i,* which is made up of two characters—the character for *sound* and the character for *heart*—so an idea is something that makes a sound in the heart (the heart in Japanese, as in Hebrew, being the seat of intelligence as well as the seat of feeling).
>
> Isn't that a wonderful picture? There is something lying deep within you that suddenly one day without warning sets off an alarm, rings, sounds, waking up your heart. (1989, 28)

The second image likens the process of writing fiction to "a grain of sand that keeps rubbing at your vitals until you find you are building a coating around it" (1981, 26). Developing the image, Paterson writes:

> I am conscious of feeding the process, though even this is indirect. I read, I think, I talk, I look, I listen, I hate, I fear, I love, I weep, and somehow all of my life gets wrapped around the grain. I don't get a perfect pearl every time, but then, neither does the oyster. (1981, 26)

A third image compares the fiction writer with a spider—"their lives hanging by a thread spun out of their own guts" (1981, 60). Both the fiction writer and the spider "take that fragile thread and weave it into a pattern" (1981, 61).

A fourth image is the writer or artist as "The Crane Wife" (1989, 71–72). In this story a wounded crane returns as a young woman who "sets up a loom," "closes it off with sliding paper doors," and asks her husband never to look in on her while she is weaving (1989, 71). While the fabric the woman weaves is exquisitely beautiful, the weaving leaves her more and more exhausted. Finally overcome by curiosity and greed, her husband, Yohei, pulls back the door: "What Yohei saw was not human. It was a crane, smeared with blood, for with its beak it had plucked out its own feathers to place them in the loom."[4] Commenting on this story's meaning for her, Paterson writes, "That is what art is all about. It is weaving fabric from the feathers you have plucked from your own breast" (1989, 72).[5]

Two threads in these images of the writing process link them with the personal dimension of conversational preaching. One is that writing begins with something that "impinges on my own life" (1989, 104)—"a sound in the heart," "a grain of sand that keeps rubbing at your vitals" (1981, 26), or "an uneasy feeling in the pit of my stomach" (1989, 92). These descriptions are images of the trouble, disequilibrium, or ambiguity that sets a sermonic plot on its journey.

A second thread is "that the only raw material I have for the stories I tell lies deep within myself" (1989, 137). For Paterson, our own lives are our only "entrance into the sum of human experience" (1981, 47):

> I do not pretend, nor do I know any writers who do, to have a monopoly on Truth. I can only see the human experience through the one pair of eyes I have been given. I can only tell the truth as I, with all my sins and limitations, can apprehend it. (1981, 107)

Writers, therefore, must be content with "little truths" (1981, 18), with whatever "vision I have right now" to which " I must be as faithful as I can" (1989, 36). Again, the intersection between my understanding of conversational preaching and fiction writing as Paterson describes it is this autobiographical dimension of both. Because absolute truth is inaccessible, we preachers must be content with "little truths" (Paterson 1981, 18), which are partial and personal.

Because conversational preaching, like fiction writing, is inseparable from "autobiography" (Paterson 1989, 8; see also 78), it is dependent on the multiple conversations that broaden and enlarge these "little truths," variously imaged as sounds in the heart, grains-of-sand-turning-into pearls, spider webs, or crane-weavings. I resonate with Elisabeth Schüssler Fiorenza's insistence that, because the preacher's experiences and articulations are never universal and normative, they need the corrective of the multiple experiences of God's people (1983, 45, 49, 52). In the process of sermon making, I must place my private articulations of my personal experiences in conversation with those who can enlarge and reconfigure them. My hope is that my preaching will awaken, give voice to, echo, encourage, or validate sounds in both my own heart and the hearts of the worshipers, particularly where those sounds have been disvalued, muffled, or extinguished. This personal dimension of conversational preaching funds its communal dimension: as my deepest experiences and convictions are touched, validated, and invited out of their hiding-places, I become able to articulate more confidently the wealth of my experiences, reflections, and wagers. I thus become a more self-confident participant with my brothers and sisters in the church's central, life-giving conversations.

Theologian Rebecca S. Chopp (1991) also contributes to this discussion of the personal or autobiographical dimension of conversational preaching. Although she writes about women, I believe her insights apply to both men and women who resonate with conversational preaching. Chopp envisions women developing "new discourses" by exercising their power both "to write their lives" and "to speak of their multiplicity and differences, their pleasure and their tribulations, their longings and their comforts."[6] She encourages women publicly "to speak their subjectivity" (154, see 25). Each woman, she claims, should be allowed "to speak her self, her desires, her time and space, her hopes, her God" (18). Proclamation then is testimony that involves "confession of the self" and narration of "what we see and hear in relation to ultimate reality" (61).[7] Such proclamation is inseparable from "the involvement of our lives" (61). And the power of proclamation for Chopp is rooted in "speaking one's own life" (62).

I suggest that conversational preaching participates in these "new discourses" as this proclamation shaped by the stuff of our lives—the sounds in our hearts; our tears, hopes, fears, loves, desires, confessions; our glimpses, experiences, and interpretations of God. And I suspect that the passion of preaching is linked to how deeply preachers are speaking their own lives.

This personal dimension of conversational preaching, as I have revisited and augmented it through the insights of Paterson and Chopp, relates to current practices already present in certain congregations. The descriptions of the preaching of some white mainline women preachers and of *testimonios* in Protestant Hispanic churches offer data that conversational preaching needs to explore further.

Pastoral theologian Lynn N. Rhodes describes the linkage a number of white mainline clergywomen make between their preaching and their personal experiences. These descriptions highlight the potential consequences of such preaching:

> [These clergywomen] make it clear to their congregations that their own experience is the basis for their insight in preaching. This is critical for two reasons. First, they want to respect diversity of experience. "I preach out of my own experience," said one woman. "That is what I claim, and thus I say to the people in the congregation, 'That is what I expect from you; not conformity to my ideas but honest reflection upon your own experience.'"
>
> Second, it is important to these women to preach experientially to tell people that the source of authority is embodied in one's life. "When I first came, the complaints about my sermons were that they were too emotional and personal. But," says this woman, "I continued to preach that way until the people in my congregation began to see that what I was doing was affirming their right to reflect seriously upon their own faith experience." Since that time, people in her congregation have begun to reflect upon and share their faith. About twenty people in the congregation have preached. The experience is empowering. Hearing their friends reflect upon their own faith and its meaning for them, people know that it is possible for them also to share their own faith, to challenge each other, and to change. . . . For this pastor, the growth in the number of "preachers" in the congregation is a sign of the authority of her own preaching. (1987, 47–48)

Conversational preaching resonates with this kind of preaching that reflects the preacher's personal experience and invites others to preach in ways that "share their own faith" and "challenge each other" (ibid.).

Conversational preaching also resonates with *testimonios,* which Martell Otero describes as "a central part of the worship experience in [Hispanic Protestant] churches" (1994, 82). *Testimonios* are "the witness of the believers [that] gives insight to the community" (82). They include "the sharing of the Word, the oral histories conserved, the give and take among the *hermanos* and *hermanas,* particularly those whose witness is considered to be sound and credible" (82). Then Martell Otero makes this important claim: "*Testimonios* can be shared precisely because it is done in the context of *la familia, la iglesia,* the community of faith" (82).

Inclusiveness

This focus on the personal dimension of conversational preaching highlights the importance of a fourth characteristic, an intentional inclusiveness. I emphasized in chapter 4 the importance of preaching's reflecting a multiplicity of experiences. There I discussed Schüssler Fiorenza's claim that the preacher's experience is never normative and therefore must be broadened and challenged by the experiences of others. Here I want to suggest three other links between the personal and the inclusive dimensions of conversational preaching.

First, by being intensely personal, conversational preaching potentially evokes the personal experiences of others. When preachers are willing to explore the depths of their own hearts and lives, worshipers are often willing to do the same. Paterson calls her readers "coauthors" who bring to their reading their own lives (1989, 37). Her hope in writing fiction for those "under the age of fourteen" (85) is not to give her readers "packaged answers" (35) or "to whip the little rascals into shape" (1981, 124), but to invite them "to go within themselves to listen to the sounds of their own hearts" (1989, 35). Sometimes readers find themselves plummeting to their "emotional and imaginative roots" where they make "connections the author herself wouldn't have dreamed of" (69). Paterson writes that "it's a wonderful feeling when readers hear what I thought I was trying to say, but there is no law that they must. Frankly, it is even more thrilling for a reader to find something in my writing that I hadn't until that moment known was there" (1981, 24; see also 1989, 15, 68).

Similarly, conversational preaching, rooted in experiences that arise from the depths of the preacher's heart and life, helps shape an ethos of safety and trust. When personal experiences are validated and encouraged, not discounted or ridiculed, worshipers begin to risk listening to and articulating the sounds deep within their own hearts, even the echoes and memories of abuse and pain. By being intentionally personal, conversational preaching is intentionally inclusive, as the preacher's personal experiences fund a wealth of personal experiences within the congregation.

A second link between the personal and the inclusive dimensions of conversational preaching is that conversational preaching seeks to reflect multiple life experiences by avoiding claims concerning what is human or universal and by cautious use of the pronoun "we."

The conversation at the homiletical table is aware of the importance of preaching's reflecting diverse experiences. But in general, the discussions there reverse claims I want to make about conversational preaching.

Many discussions in the homiletical literature describe the preacher and the congregation as being similar because of "common human experience" or "human nature" that presumably underlies diversity. The assumption seems to be that the preacher and the congregation are different because of the preacher's superior understanding of truth or the gospel, interpretation of scripture, of faith experience, which—being more biblical, more theologically sound, or perhaps simply more faithful—should be transferred to the congregation.

Conversational preaching reverses these claims. The similarity between the preacher and the worshipers is a modicum of faith and commitment within a community of faith. The differences lie in divergent life experiences out of which arise a variety of interpretations and wagers. I am not claiming there is unanimity within any congregation about matters of faith and practice. I am claiming that any given community has at some level a "shared way of understanding and interpreting reality" and "a common paradigm or interpretive framework for what constitutes legitimate authority" (Russell 1993, 39). Conversational preaching takes place within a worshiping community where some degree of shared faith and commitment gives rise to the worshipers' sense of being a household of God or an ecclesial family. Within this community of shared faith and commitment, conversational preaching seeks to acknowledge a diversity of experiences, interpretations, and wagers, especially those on the margins without power, status, or voice.

Conversational preaching tries to take seriously the dangers inherent in claims about "common human experience" and "human nature." These dangers include a blindness to conflicting experiences and a resultant imperialism that names as "common" or "human" what is particular and limited. There may be some experiences that are common to all humans. But often statements about "common human experience" ignore or dismiss contrary evidence, and often "facts" about "human nature" characterize only a segment, many times a dominant segment, of humanity. Those who are marginal or outside the norm are the first to recognize just how particular and limited such statements and "facts" are.

Feminists have undercut many claims about "common human experience" and "human nature" by exposing their masculine bias. Shifting from what is "human," they have turned their attention to describing "women's experience."

This new naming, however, has been equally imperialistic because, again, of claims to universality. Black womanist ethicist Jacquelyn Grant accuses white feminists of racism because they ignore differences between their own experiences and those of African-American women (1989). White feminists presume to define as "women's experience" (198, 199) what is particular to their own "bourgeois" (204), privileged position (see 200). By doing this, they imitate all oppressors who "define the rules and then solicit others to play the game" (200). Thus they retain "the power of definition and control" (199–200) in the women's movement.

As one who has profoundly benefited from feminist writings and who needs to listen carefully to Grant's accusations, I am aware, at least to some extent, of my participation in the efforts of my privileged culture to cling to "the power of definition and control" (ibid.). At the same time, Grant encourages me to call into question all claims to common experience and universality. I remember how often I have listened to a preacher describing what "we" do or feel or think, and I was aware that the statements might reflect the preacher's reality but they did not reflect mine; "I" was not included in the preacher's "we."

Conversational preaching seeks to avoid claims about what is common, universal, or human by acknowledging both its own particularity and the diversity of other experiences. Because conversational preaching is rooted in the preacher's personal experience, it acknowledges the legitimacy of others' experiences. Aware that personal experience is inseparable from interpretations and faith claims, conversational preaching urges preachers to say "I" when referring to personal experiences and wagers, to be cautious and deliberate about saying "we," and to make spacious room for the experiences of others, specifically those who hover at the margins of one's known reality. Respect for the multiplicity of experiences among all people and especially the people of God goes hand in hand with conversational preaching's personal and particular character.

A third link joins the personal and the inclusive dimensions of conversational preaching. Conversational preaching welcomes a variety of personal responses to every sermon. Many communities of faith include either within the worship service or afterward opportunities for reflection and personal sharing. These communities model ways of legitimizing a variety of personal experiences, interpretations, and convictions as primary ingredients in the community's ongoing conversations.

Schüssler Fiorenza suggests that a time for discussion should follow the sermon, because "after lectures we have responses, after press-conferences we have questions" (1983, 49). When worshipers have regular opportunities to raise questions or concerns, give voice to thoughts and experiences evoked by the sermon, or pursue conflicting interpretations, especially those offered by or on behalf of the marginal and the silenced, their voices are valued and nurtured. These occasions for response also place the sermon, usually voiced by one person, expressly within the larger ecclesial conversations.

Response times after sermons were widespread in the churches of New England during the early seventeenth century (Adams 1981). After the sermon the preacher sat down, and the members of the congregation, usually male, asked questions of the preacher or spoke "a word of Exhortation to the people."[8] In some towns women were allowed to exhort but not to ask questions; in others they were prohibited in public worship from doing either. This practice of exhortations and questions in worship was particularly widespread in the Bay Colony as "witnessed by assembly resolutions and sermons aimed to regulate such practice" (29). Although I do not favor the blatant sexual discrimination of this earlier practice, which undermines an ethos of trust and safety, I do favor an official forum time either within the service of worship or immediately thereafter as an opportunity for worshipers to voice their personal responses to the sermon.

Two potential problems deserve attention. On the one hand, I do not mean to imply that the preacher is limited to personal stories or to the repeated use of the pronoun "I." What is autobiographical and personal is at the core of preaching, but it is always broadened, reworked, and weaved into sermons along with the experiences of others so that what characterizes the preacher melds with what characterizes others. On the other hand, I do not mean to imply that every personal experience or wager should be acceptable within every community of faith. The community does and should continue to set and reset its standards by means of its multiple conversations, including the divine-human ones.

The Conversation
with Scripture

This brings me to a fifth and final dimension of conversational preaching: scriptural. Because I take my own personal experiences seriously, as well as the experiences of others, I also take Scripture seriously as the record of the experiences of our foremothers and forefathers who wrestled with God and with what it meant to live as God's people. Because I take the human-human conversations seriously, including those with our deepest selves, I also take the divine-human conversations seriously, including those with biblical texts. In these conversations, biblical texts offer not only what is agreeable and familiar but also what is divergent, challenging, and Other; and in these conversations we are invited not only to *listen*, but also to speak, question, and probe.

Listening to texts is a major topic at the homiletical table. What is sometimes missing there is a deep valuing of the readers as anything other than discerners of an encoded Word or receivers of a divine message. The readers' voices are often silenced, their lives and experiences bracketed out. In addition, traditional and kerygmatic voices at the homiletical table tend to reduce the Otherness, the mysterious elusiveness of the scriptural witness, to a known truth or a formulaic *kerygma*.

No conversation is possible without at least two partners, each of whom brings "particular concerns and unique experiences and questions" (Browning 1994, 131). Conversational preaching seeks to nurture the reading of Scripture as a conversation between the community of faith and texts about matters of ultimate importance—our relationships with God, one another, and the world for which Jesus died, which God continues to love, and which is branded with God's promise of shalom.

Rebecca S. Chopp describes the relationship between the community of faith and Scripture as one of mutual interpretation (1991). Texts should never be read as though they were mirrors for the readers' already-known stories (64). Instead, Chopp claims that interpretation is a dialogue between the reader and the text in which each "respects the historicity" of the other (8), "between text and experience" in which neither seeks "to translate the one into the other" (46). What is important is "the back and forth movement of the text with us as readers/proclaimers, in the radical otherness of the text that is in front of us, and within our experience as different from the text" (58). Interpretation's goal is "to enrich both [participants] through the ongoing dialogue—a dialogue of openness—between the two" (46). This "back and forth movement" between Scripture and "readers/proclaimers" (58) takes place within the "inclusive" (93) or "dialogical community" (95). Such a community has learned "to reason together, to deliberate its ongoing practices" (92). In such a community, through "ongoing discourse and dialogue, the freedom to speak is nourished and strengthened" (95).

And so we have come full circle. Always at the heart of conversational preaching is the experience of connectedness, the sense of community and mutual interdependence, of trust and safety, that allows all participants to speak out of their personal experiences, interpretations, and wagers.

I have tried to describe the broad brushstrokes of conversational preaching as I have discerned them both within and outside the homiletical literature. The questions remain, inviting others to join the probing: So what *is* conversational preaching as a practice that already exists? Who is preaching this way and reflecting on it as an alternative way of preaching? My provisionary interpretations seek the interpretations of others. My proposal seeks the echoing or contrapuntal proposals of others. And because these are my wagers, they are undeniably limited and partisan, dependent on others for broader vision.

Notes

Notes to Introduction

1. My proposal for a conversational understanding of preaching shares these characteristics in common with John McClure's collaborative preaching. He characterizes collaborative preaching as "a communal event," "no privileged voice" (1995, 51), and "a process with a purpose" (52). I also resonate with his description of preaching as "an open process" in which "there is no closure to the homiletical conversation" (52). I am uncomfortable with his continued use of the word "persuasion" to describe preaching's purpose and ecclesial leadership. Persuasive preaching and leadership styles have been abusive to many in the church whose experiences and convictions have been consistently ignored or dismissed. I realize that McClure's collaborative method works against such abuse, but continued use of the word is potentially dangerous in sanctioning previous definitions and practices.

At least two differences distinguish my conversational preaching from McClure's collaborative preaching. One is that he envisions the relationship between the preacher and the worshipers as that of "beloved strangers" who work out together how the community is to live (54). In conversational preaching, their relationship is more like that of "cohorts" (53), a designation McClure rejects. A second difference is that McClure focuses on a sermonic form by which the sermon reflects the journey of the pre-sermon discussion group. While this is a possible form for conversational preaching if the content is offered as a provisional interpretation or proposal, this particular form diminishes the personal dimension that I believe is a major component of conversational preaching as an actual practice. See chapter 5 for a discussion of the personal dimension of conversational preaching.

2. These are, listed chronologically, James W. Cox, *Preaching* (San Francisco: Harper & Row, 1985); Fred B. Craddock, *Preaching* (Nashville: Abingdon Press, 1985); Deane A. Kemper, *Effective Preaching: A Manual for Students and Pastors* (Philadelphia: Westminster Press, 1985); John Killinger, *Fundamentals of Preaching* (Philadelphia: Fortress Press, 1985); Ian Pitt-Watson, *A Primer for Preachers* (Grand Rapids: Baker Book House, 1986); Ronald E. Sleeth, *Proclaiming the Word* (Nashville: Abingdon Press, 1986); David G. Buttrick, *Homiletic: Moves and Structures* (Philadelphia: Fortress Press, 1987); Clyde E. Fant, *Preaching for Today*, rev. ed. (San Francisco: Harper & Row, 1987); Thomas G. Long, *The Witness of Preaching* (Louisville: Westminster/John Knox Press, 1989); Don M. Wardlaw, ed., *Learning Preaching: Understanding and Participating in the Process* (Lincoln, Ill.: The Academy of Homiletics, Lincoln Christian College and Seminary Press, 1989).

3. Many influences account for this disappearance of homiletical consensus. Seen with a wide-angle lens, homiletical theory is here reflecting the larger

world of scholarship where many of the former consensuses were losing their following. Jean-François Lyotard voices the conviction, or lament, of many scholars, artists, scientists, students, and others: "Consensus is a horizon that is never reached" (1984, 61). In fact, for many "consensus has become an outmoded and suspect value" (66). This suspicion arose particularly among those outside the power structures who recognized that a consensus always represents the agreements of the dominant culture. As various groups outside the white power structures began to make their voices heard, the former consensuses as pillars that kept these power structures in place began to crumble. The consensual "grand narratives" have given way to "little narratives" (60). This shift to "little narratives" is also reflected in homiletical theory, as seen with a close-up lens. For example, in a paper for the 1979 Academy of Homiletics meeting whose theme was "Preaching and Story," Arthur Van Seters claims that "the 'what' of preaching, the history, theology, biblical basis, or whatever else"—those agreements that had grounded the Broadus and the Davis consensuses—are not necessarily the starting point for teaching students to preach; instead he suggests beginning with "the students themselves, their stories, their persons, who they uniquely are" ("The Preacher's Own Story as Integral to Preaching the Torah/Jesus Story," *Preaching and Story* [Academy of Homiletics, meeting at Cabrini Contact Center, Des Plaines, Ill., Dec. 8–9, 1991], 8).

4. Others make similar claims regarding the word *conversation.* In "Hackshem," an address delivered at the Opening Convocation of Columbia Theological Seminary, September 16, 1992, Dean R. Kevin LaGree, of the Candler School of Theology of Emory University, made the following remarks about the late British philosopher Michael Oakeshott:

> For Oakeshott, conversation was a way people learned and existed that was "non-hierarchical, non-directive, and non-assertive." He wrote: "In a conversation the participants are not engaged in an inquiry or a debate; there is no 'truth' to be discovered, no proposition to be proved, no conclusion sought. They are not concerned to inform, to persuade, or refute one another, and therefore the cogency of their utterance does not depend upon their all speaking the same idiom; they may differ without disagreeing." (2, quoted in Martin E. Marty, ed., *Context: A Commentary on the Interaction of Religion and Culture,* 25 [August 15, 1991]: 3)

5. Letty M. Russell acknowledges a similar hope: "My goal is to talk about the church in such a way that those who read this book from a Christian feminist perspective can say, 'Yes, I recognize this as the church for which I long, and for which I struggle" (1993, 14).

Notes to Chapter 1.
Homiletics' Elder Statesman Speaks

1. This version of "Cinderella" is recorded by the Brothers Grimm. See *The Complete Fairy Tales of the Brothers Grimm,* trans. Jack Zipes (Toronto and New York: Bantam Books, 1987), 86–92. The Greek story of Procrustes, a giant who

forced travelers to fit into his bed, was a gift from Linda Sherer, a former student at Columbia Theological Seminary. She reminded me that sometimes the experience of women being taught to preach is not self-mutilation, as in the Cinderella story, but violence, as in the Procrustes story. The self-mutilation and violence, albeit unintentional, will continue as long as a single voice tries to dominate the homiletical table insisting it is the only option for everyone who preaches.

2. Katie G. Cannon's discussions of the role of Black women's literature, stories, and art in transmitting their "moral wisdom" challenges me to probe more deeply my discomfort associated with the concept of transmission (*Black Womanist Ethics,* American Academy of Religion Academy Series, ed. Susan Thistlethwaite, no. 60 [Atlanta: Scholars Press, 1988], 4). According to Cannon, Black women write not only to inspire but also to teach (85) and to inform (90). These writers "implicitly pass on and receive from one generation to the next moral formulas for survival that allow them to stand over against the perversions of ethics and morality imposed on them by whites and males who support racial imperialism in a patriarchal social order" (7). These women therefore "function as continuing symbolic conveyors and transformers of the values acknowledged by the female members of the Black Community" (7–8).

Cannon's positive assessment of the transmission of formulas in the "Black female community" (6) clarifies the twofold nature of my discomfort with transmission as a concept in homiletical theory. First, I have resisted what has felt like an exclusive claim that all preaching should aim, as its primary goal, to transmit truth or a kerygmatic formula that has ignored my experiences and those of others like me; for example, many women. Second, I have resisted the sometimes overt, sometimes subtle, implication that the preacher knows the truth and should transmit it to the worshipers, who remain ignorant until enlightened by the sermon. The Black women writers Cannon describes are never so isolated from community. Rather, the values, "moral counsel" (4), or "moral formulas" (2) they transmit are rooted in communal life and "acknowledged by the female members of the Black community" (8; see also 5, 9, 151). Although I continue to be wary of transmission because of its accompanying "temptation to imperialism" (Craddock 1974, 65), nevertheless I am intrigued by Cannon's positive assessment of transmission among oppressed people. Transmission of a people's inherited wisdom is a necessary strategy for survival. I am challenged to continue rethinking the relationship between preaching and transmission. At the same time, I will continue to value my conviction that much of the preaching that has aimed to transmit the church's inherited wisdom has been oppressive to many people because the mode of transmission has been imperialistic and the conversations that defined the inherited wisdom have often excluded the voices of the powerless, women, racial and ethnic minorities, and other oppressed peoples.

3. Harold Freeman, for example, claims that "persuasive communication must sometimes be a two-way street" (1987, 89). In other words, the occasional two-directional dimension of preaching is in service of one-directional "persuasive communication."

Similarly, James W. Cox (1985) describes various congregational responses to a sermon that create a "dialogue" between the congregation and the preacher in which "words and feelings begin to fly back and forth" (51). His conclusion to this section, however, delineates the congregation's options: "faith and obedience" or "unbelief and disobedience to the message" (51).

4. I want to distinguish between the word *proposition* as a technical homiletical term for the key sentence on which a sermon is built and the word *propositional*. James W. Cox (1985) explicitly avoids the word *proposition* in the former sense. My use of *propositional* here refers to the definition of a proposition as "something that is expressed in a statement, as opposed to the way it is expressed" (*The American Heritage Dictionary* [2d College ed.]). Truth that is "expressed in a statement" is propositional.

5. The conviction that the gist of every sermon should be stated in a single sentence is not restricted to traditional theory. It was, however, an important component of Broadus and Weatherspoon's homiletical theory and remains one of the legacies of traditional homiletics that is hardest to break. I am not advocating that all preachers should abandon this rule. I do describe in chapter 4 one form of preaching that finds its unity and coherence not in a single idea but in a plot.

6. I use the word *gap* in a very particular sense here. It describes the explicit or implicit distance that separates the preacher and the congregation in most descriptions of preaching. Rebecca S. Chopp discusses a different sense of the word. She writes of those gaps that allow God to move in human life, that make transformation possible, and that exist "within all relations" (1991, 59). For Chopp, gaps allow for difference and otherness, which in turn allow for both real solidarity, as opposed to enforced unanimity, and transformation.

Because of Chopp's insights I have probed deeper my negative appraisal of the gap between the preacher and the congregation. I continue to contend that conversational preaching begins in solidarity, equality, and mutuality; it is grounded in the priesthood of all believers and their partnership in the gospel. But, presupposing connectedness, it opens the door to and invites differences. Within the community of faith, no two believers are identical. Conversational preaching acknowledges differences in experiences, interpretations, and convictions among worshipers who nevertheless constitute to varying degrees a community of faith.

7. These claims are found in Gilligan (1982, 2), Belenky and others (1986, 102–103), and West (1988, 70–71).

8. In describing this alternative developmental journey, Gilligan (1982) relies heavily on the work of Nancy Chodorow, who described the formation of personality in children under three, and Janet Lever, who identified different patterns of socialization in middle-class girls and boys aged ten and eleven. Gilligan's own research involved three studies: one with college students, one with pregnant women, and one with a range of participants from age six to sixty.

9. Gilligan's contributions are, first, the collecting of data that challenges Erikson's schema, and second, the formulating of the fundamental themes that distinguish these two distinct developmental journeys. Carol Franz and Kathleen White

have developed an alternative set of developmental stages based on the theme of attachment. Their attachment pathway is summarized and slightly modified by Carroll Saussy in *The Gift of Anger: A Call to Faithful Action* (Louisville: Westminster John Knox Press, 1995), 41–43.

10. Gilligan 1982, 7–8, citing Nancy Chodorow, *The Reproduction of Mothering* (Berkeley: University of California Press, 1978), 150, 166–67.

11. Belenky and others 1986, citing Paulo Freire, *Pedagogy of the Oppressed* (New York: Seaview, 1971), 63.

12. Brown, Clinard, and Northcutt 1963, 30, citing Samuel M. Shoemaker, *The Church Alive* (New York: E. P. Dutton & Co., 1950), 63.

13. The staying power of this conviction—that a sermon should communicate a message or an idea—is evident in the report of a survey, conducted by Baylor University in 1993, titled "Dimensions of Effective Preaching." Professors of homiletics in the United States, Canada, Great Britain, Australia, New Zealand, and South Africa were asked to list criteria necessary for effective preaching. The 140 responses "produced more than 700 criteria which have been categorized into one of seven dimensions of effective preaching" (Letter from Herbert H. Reynolds, President of Baylor University, January 31, 1994). The report lists the seven "dimensions" and includes descriptive quotations from the responses under each. "Sermon structure" is one "dimension." The description reads in part: "The effective preacher preaches sermons which are structured with a clear introduction, main body, and conclusion; all of which reflect *a central theme or focus.* The sermon is organized in a 'logical style that progressively builds *the main argument or proposition* of the sermon'" (my italics). The blurb about "Effective Communication" includes the following: "The effective preacher preaches sermons which clearly communicate *the central idea* through use of simple language and illustrations so as to convince the listeners of the message" (my italics).

14. Semmelroth 1965, 246, citing Max Picard, *Der Mensch und das Wort* (Zürich: n.p., 1955), 35; English translation, *Man and Language* (Chicago: n.p., 1963).

Notes to Chapter 2.
Kerygmatic Theory States Its Claims

1. Mounce 1960, 154, citing Gustaf Wingren, *Predikan; en principiel studie* (n.p., n.d.), 296, quoted by E. Jerome Johanson, *Theology Today* 7 (October 1951): 356.

2. Henry Mitchell's *Black Preaching* (1979) was originally published in 1970. In his later books, *The Recovery of Preaching* (1977) and *Celebration and Experience in Preaching* (Nashville: Abingdon Press, 1990), his kerygmatic understanding of preaching overlaps with transformational views of preaching described in chapter 3.

3. Barth 1963a, 747, citing Martin Luther, "Wider Hans Worst. 1541," in *D. Martin Luthers Werke, Kritische Gesamtausgabe,* vol. 51 (Weimer: Hermann Böhlaus Nachfolger, 1914), 516.

4. Worshipers and preachers also struggle with this high expectation that the sermon should be an event. Willard Francis Jabusch describes the disappointment of the person in the pew:

The Christian . . . has wanted the spoken word . . . to be a means of establishing communion with Jesus Christ. He has wanted at least some of the
preaching that he hears to be a prayer, that is, to bring him to contact with
Jesus and his heavenly Father. . . . He still hopes that at least the preaching
word will reach out to him, drawing him closer to his brothers and sisters
and to his Savior, freeing him from his isolation, the coldness of his heart,
and the heaviness of his thoughts. So often he has been disappointed. . . .
Rising expectations on the part of a more critical audience have outstripped
the preaching performance. (1980, 27)

Some pastors also feel disappointed, aware that they fall short of their own high
hopes for preaching. A pastor-colleague lamented, "I proclaim the Word of God
so hearers and ultimately the world can be transformed. The Word of God is powerful; it is transformative. I believe it can change congregations. The Word
preached faithfully over time can make a difference." Then the pastor added, "It
can be discouraging when it seems like nothing is happening."
    5. C. H. Dodd, *The Parables of the Kingdom,* 3rd ed. (New York: Charles Scrib-
ner's Sons, 1936), 204, quoted in Thompson (1962, 143).

Notes to Chapter 3.
Transformational Voices Enter the Conversation

    1. David Cairns, for example, who is an advocate of kerygmatic theory, de-
scribes his confidence in theology's ability to provide the norm for preaching: "Theology is thus meant to be a norm for preaching, but it is itself subject to another
norm, the revelation of God in Christ. Its aim is to keep preaching true to the revelation of God" (*A Gospel Without Myth?: Bultmann's Challenge to the Preacher*
[London: SCM Press, 1960], 17).
    2. David Mark Greenhaw's Ph.D. dissertation, "Creative preaching: An alternate
metaphor for the function of preaching" (Drew University, 1987), claims that, by
creating "the expectation of a new future" (54), "preaching creates communities
that anticipate a world, a possible world, the world of the eschaton" (119; see 54,
139–40).
    3. Although the new hermeneutic "had a somewhat short life" in American the-
ology (John Macquarrie, *Twentieth-Century Religious Thought,* 4th ed. [Philadel-
phia: Trinity Press International, 1988], 391), it has had a long and fruitful life in
homiletics.
    4. Keir 1962, 65, citing Austin Farrer, *The Glass of Vision* (London: n.p., 1948),
lecture iv.
    5. Ibid., lecture vi.
    6. Schüssler Fiorenza 1983, 45. She illustrates her charge:

Quite often I have heard sermons about the insecurity wrought among the
faithful by Vatican II, where it was obvious that the problem was not that of
the congregation but that of the preacher. . . . I have patiently listened to di-
atribes against the desire for power, the lust after pride; sermons that may
reflect male drives and sins but do not take into account the need of women

to take control over their own lives or to be encouraged in their search for self-affirmation. I have listened to sermon after sermon denouncing our consumerist attitudes and self-serving wealth, sermons addressing the upper middle class members of the congregation but not those who struggle for economic survival. A homilist who has just returned suntanned from a vacation in Florida or Arizona is ill equipped to preach against the consumerism of a suburban housewife who has not had a vacation in years. (1983, 46)

7. Fiction writer Katherine Paterson, based on her experiences as a missionary in Japan, came to a similar conclusion—"a conclusion that linguists now advance: language is not simply the instrument by which we communicate thought. The language we speak will shape the thoughts and feelings themselves" (1981, 8). Remembering her frustrating attempts to communicate in Japanese when she knew only a few words, she describes her conviction at the time, "If only you could know me in *English,* you would see at once what a clever, delightful person I am" (1981, 7). Returning to her parents and sisters in the United States four years later, she recalls a different conviction:

"These people," I would say to myself, meaning my own family, "these people don't even know me." The reason I thought my family didn't know me was that they didn't know me in Japanese.

You see, in those four years I had become a different person. I had not only learned new ways to express myself, I had new thoughts to express. (8)

Language both enables and limits thinking and expression. Thus, language as "that which makes it possible for us to seek truths about the universe and about ourselves has within itself the guarantee that we will never be able to find the Truth" (11).

8. Living with the ambiguity means that I believe God is an active presence in the world. At the same time I also believe that every interpretation of God's presence and activity by individuals or communities of faith participates in human sinfulness that is in part reflected in the limitations and distortions of language.

9. I am indebted to my colleague at Columbia Theological Seminary, Charles L. Campbell, for the insight that many of the discussions of preaching as a transforming event are rooted in the study of parables.

10. Browne, 1958, 30, citing T. S. Eliot, *Selected Prose,* ed. John Hayward (n.p.: Penguin Books, 1953), 63.

Notes to Chapter 4.
Marginal Voices Crowd Around the Table

1. The idea that preaching should help people make sense of their lives was brought into the mainstream of homiletical thinking by Clement Welsh (1974). According to Welsh, the preacher functions to help "the listener to make religious sense of his universe" (32–33; see also 16, 46). Welsh's definition of preaching as "sense-making" was picked up by several other homiletical scholars. Three who acknowledge their indebtedness to Welsh are O. C. Edwards in *The Living and Active Word: One Way to Preach from the Bible Today* (New York: Seabury Press,

1975); J. Randall Nichols in both *Building the Word: The Dynamics of Communication and Preaching* (San Francisco: Harper & Row, 1980) and *The Restoring
Word* (1987); and George W. Swank (1981).

Prior to Robert E. C. Browne (1958), Harry Emerson Fosdick described his
method for preaching similarly:

> [This method] makes a sermon a cooperative enterprise between the preach-
> er and his congregation. When a man has got hold of a real difficulty in the
> life and thinking of his people and is trying to meet it, he finds himself not
> so much dogmatically thinking for them as cooperatively thinking with them.
> His sermon is an endeavor to put himself in their places and help them to
> think their way through. (Lionel Crocker, comp. and ed., *Harry Emerson Fos-
> dick's Art of Preaching: An _ 'thology* [Springfield, Ill.: Charles C. Thomas,
> 1971], 33)

2. This image of the preacher and the congꞇᵤ.'on sharing in discussion together reappears time and again in the homiletical literature after 1960. In all of
this literature, a gap continues to separate the preacher and the congregation.
For example, Reuel L. Howe describes the laity, but not the preacher, as
learners:

> The findings and conclusions of these study groups are indispensable for the
> preacher. For example, no one can really preach "justification by grace
> through faith" who has not engaged with laymen in the process by which
> laymen move in their discussion from dependence on the law for their jus-
> tification, work through their first impressions of grace as foolishness, and
> come finally to a new freedom because of it. (*Partners in Preaching: Clergy
> and Laity in Dialogue* [New York: Seabury Press, 1967], 95)

In Dietrich Ritschl's image, the preacher and the church members are learners
together (1960). Ritschl's preacher is not listening to the congregation in order to
lead them into deeper insight she or he already understands; nor is she or he seeking ways to package the sermon's preconceived message or experience for better
receptivity. Ritschl's preacher learns with and from the congregation.

John S. McClure (1995) develops a method of preaching that grows out of the
kind of nonhierarchical discussion group Ritschl describes. McClure suggests that
the sermon itself reflect the major components of the discussion's movement toward meaning.

3. Several homiletical scholars prior to Joseph Fichtner (1981) describe a relationship between preaching and the concept of conversation. Two are Gene E.
Bartlett and Rudolf Bohren.

Bartlett uses the word to describe three different activities: the discussion going
on between the church and the secular world (1962, 35–36), the "inner conversations" going on within every individual (84), and the dialogue between the believer
and God (103). Bartlett claims that preaching should enter into each of these
conversations.

Rudolf Bohren writes not only that the Word draws people into conversation
(1965, 61) but also that "a sermon becomes a conversation" when the preacher un-

derstands the hearers (57). Bohren's development of the former idea contributes nothing new to the discussion of the Word and the church by Ritschl (1960). And Bohren does not develop the latter idea.

4. Three homiletical scholars who, prior to Swank, significantly develop the relationship between preaching and dialogue are Reuel L. Howe, Henry H. Mitchell, and Alvin J. Porteous. None, however, shifts preaching away from kerygmatic homiletical theory. In *Partners in Preaching: Clergy and Laity in Dialogue* (New York: Seabury, 1967), Howe's "dialogical preaching" serves the larger purpose of an encounter (42) that enables "the Word of God to take flesh in the lives of men and women" (46). Mitchell discusses the relationship between preaching and "real dialogue" (1979, 97): preaching requires both "talk about something we can enter into" (101) and "close identity" between the preacher and the congregation (103). However, Mitchell's larger understanding of preaching remains kerygmatic. See my discussion of Mitchell in chapter 2. Alvin J. Porteous develops an understanding of preaching based on the insights of Howe and Black liberation theologians (1979). He suggests that the aim of preaching is to foster a dialogical community that can engage in critical reflection (91). In this suggestion he comes close to the understanding that I propose here. At the same time, Porteous's descriptions of preaching as a liberating event (60) and his interest in discerning "the essentials of the Christian message" (35) link him with kerygmatic views of preaching.

5. Schüssler Fiorenza's (1983) suggestions here are not entirely new. A number of homiletical scholars insist that the preacher should remember the variety of people in the congregation—for example, differences in age, temperaments, and life experiences. See, for example, James Wright (1958, 43–58). Ronald J. Allen (*Preaching for Growth* [St. Louis, Mo.: CBP Press, 1988], 49–52) proposes a grid that highlights differences in age, on the one hand, and social location, on the other. In terms of the latter, Allen includes men, women, Blacks, whites, Asian Americans, Hispanics, middle class, and lower class (52). Schüssler Fiorenza expands these categories by reminding preachers of a growing body of research that indicates that all humans do not learn, process information, or make decisions in the same way. See, for example, Gilligan (1982) and Belenky and others (1986).

6. My conviction is that not only male homilists but also male teachers of preaching should pay attention to the experiences of women and the scholarship that seeks to reflect on those experiences. Although several homiletical scholars summarize selected writings of feminist scholars, the convictions of these women do not seem to influence greatly the views of preaching being advocated. Homiletical scholars who tip their hat to feminist scholarship prior to 1990 include Clyde E. Fant (*Preaching for Today,* rev. ed. [San Francisco: Harper & Row, 1987], 57–63, 194, 200); Sider and King (1987, 67–68), and Best (1988, 116–20). Only Christine M. Smith (1989) seeks to reconstruct homiletical theory from an explicitly feminist perspective. Beardslee and others (1989) acknowledge the issues women raise for preaching and also begin to rethink preaching in new directions. See my summary of Beardslee and others in chapter 4. Two other scholars who suggest new directions for preaching based on issues that include gender are Patricia Wilson-Kastner (1989) and William K. McElvaney (1989).

7. The importance of paying particular attention to interpretations that are different from one's own is also addressed by Wayne C. Booth. In his lecture "Does the Study of Rhetoric Lead to Religion?" (delivered at the Candler School of Theology of Emory University as part of the Franklin Parker Lectureship in Preaching, 19 February, 1986, cassette), Booth claims:

> But the genuine spirit of rhetorical inquiry says . . . your opponents' views almost certainly have more to be said for them than you have yet discovered. Your own views certainly, not *almost* certainly, but certainly, have more to be said against them, more to be said of their limitations, than you have yet realized. The best truth you can hope for out of any encounter will thus be a dialectical truth emerging from the encounter, a truth different from what either of you began with, and that truth in turn, you can be certain, will still be fragmentary, partial, limited, in need of further dialogue, further dialectical modifications and so on.

Booth's argument is that such an understanding of rhetoric leads one to religion because it presupposes *the* truth. This truth however "remains forever elusive" (ibid.).

8. Thomas J. Mickey's dissertation is *Role Conflict for the Preacher: A Study in Communication and Religion* (University of Iowa, December, 1979). It is summarized in the Appendix to Fichtner (1981), 159–64.

9. The exception is David Buttrick's *Homiletic: Moves and Structures* (1987) where the goal of preaching is transformation of congregational consciousness.

10. I first appropriated the word "wager" from Paul Ricoeur:

> Hermeneutics . . . requires that the philosopher wager his belief, and that he lose or win the wager by putting the revealing power of the symbol to the test of self-understanding. In understanding himself better, the philosopher verifies, up to a certain point, the wager of his faith. (*The Symbolism of Evil*, trans. Emerson Buchanan [Boston: Beacon Press, 1967], 308)

Martin Marty describes the preacher as inviting the congregation to a wager (*The Word: People Participating in Preaching* [Philadelphia: Fortress Press, 1984], 74).

11. Thompson 1962, 25, citing Alfred North Whitehead (*Religion in the Making* [New York: The Macmillan Co., 1926], 56).

12. The revised edition of this classic is titled *The Liberating Pulpit* (Nashville: Abingdon Press, 1994).

13. This argument about collective testimony as a guarantee against self-deception could also be made for Judaism, Islam, and Buddhism.

14. Hall 1971, 86, citing Willem Zuurdeeg, *An Analytical Philosophy of Religion* (Nashville: Abingdon Press, 1958), 45.

15. I take Thielicke's understanding of the problems of language a step further than he does. I do not believe that words are *in danger* of their meanings being changed; rather, I believe that they *will inevitably* be changed through years of usage. Neither do I believe that a linguistic Eden existed where language was pure and true. Language is only pure and true where consensus is tightly controlled.

16. Thomas G. Long's discussion of the image of the preacher as witness sets the image in the context of the court trial (1989b, 42–47). The concept of truth is an important one for Long (43). I prefer a less formal understanding of the witness as one who speaks out of personal experiences and convictions in the context of the larger ecclesial conversations. Witnesses are those who in formal and informal contexts "cannot keep from speaking about what we have seen and heard" (Acts 4:20).

17 Scott 1985, 17. Here Scott is following a number of scholars, themselves indebted to Ferdinand de Saussure, who distinguish between a sign (or the signifier) and that to which the sign refers (or the signified). See Saussure, *Course in General Linguistics,* ed. Charles Bally and Albert Sechehaye in collaboration with Albert Reidlinger, trans. Wade Baskin (New York: McGraw Hill, 1966).

18. I have no interest in choosing sides in the debate between the "experiential-expressivist" position, represented by Paul Ricoeur and David Tracy, and the "cultural-linguistic" position, represented by Hans Frei, George Lindbeck, Stanley Hauerwas, and David Kelsey (Gary L. Comstock, "Two Types of Narrative Theology," *Journal of the American Academy of Religion* 55 [Winter 1987]: 688; the terms belong to George Lindbeck, *The Nature of Doctrine: Religion and Theology in a Postliberal Age* [Philadelphia: Westminster Press, 1984]). I believe that both positions belong within the spiral methodology described by Letty M. Russell (1993, 30–36) or within the hermeneutical circle of Latin American theologies.

19. I am not interested in taking sides in the debate about whether form mimetically represents "what is" or whether form imposes an alien order on "what is." I suppose I have made a wager that something "is." Any attempt to represent "what is" is always approximate, ambiguous, vested with the interest of the artist, and reflective of the convictions, both acknowledged and unacknowledged, of the interpreter's significant communities.

20. I knew a sculptor/poet who called his creations "refuse." What he valued was the process of creating. Having created, he was not particularly interested in the products of the process.

21. Lowry 1985, 42, citing Wesley A. Kort, *Narrative Elements and Religious Meaning* (Philadelphia: Fortress Press, 1975).

22. A former student at Columbia Theological Seminary, Kim Olson, suggested to me a sermonic form that resembles painting. What gives unity and coherence to the sermon is the single, though sometimes complex, image that is the finished painting the preacher is composing. The sermon consists of the preacher's "painting" the picture by directing the congregation's attention to the various components that make up the full image.

23. I borrow the idea of "a proper ending" from Katherine Paterson (1989, 183). Such an ending is "rooted in this earth and lean[s] in the direction of the New Jerusalem" (191). Paterson expressly denies that she is looking for solutions to problems. Human life, she insists, cannot be reduced "to a series of problems that can, with insight and a bit of doing, be solved" (31). In the same vein, she claims, "if we look at life as a series of problems needing solving, it is hard not to offer nicely packaged, portable solutions, preferably paperback" (31). Such an approach to life and writing—and I would add, preaching—results in "shallowness" (32). Instead of offering solutions, good narrative sermons—like good short stories, novels, and plays—have "proper endings."

24. Paterson likens the process of creating a work of fiction to a seed "that grows in the dark, and one day you look and there is a full-grown plant with a flower on it" (1981, 26). H. Grady Davis's description of the process reflects more conscious control than Paterson's: he compares "designing a sermon" to "*making* a plant grow to the form inherent in it" (1958, 21, my italics).

25. Paterson claims that the heart of a story is an experience, not an idea:

If you ask me what one of my stories is about, . . . I will cry out, "If I could tell you what it was about in one sentence, why would I have spent nearly three years and two hundred fifteen pages doing so?" In the writer's mind, the story is not divisible, explainable, reducible. "Some people," Flannery O'Connor says, "have the notion that you read the story and then climb out of it into the meaning, but for the fiction writer himself the whole story is the meaning, because it is an experience, not an abstraction." (Paterson 1989, 134, citing Flannery O'Connor, "The Nature and Aim of Fiction," *Mystery and Manners,* ed. Sally and Robert Fitzgerald [New York: Farrar, Straus, & Giroux, 1969], 73)

26. I use the word *rechart* with care. The original journey is not replicated or recreated. Rather, the original journey, through its meaning for the interpreter and its significant components in the interpreter's memory, provides the raw materials for subsequent journeys. Each subsequent journey, however, is in fact a new journey for both the preacher and the worshipers.

27. Katherine Paterson illustrates the power of a work of fiction to generate a variety of meanings. She describes the meaning of the story "The Crane Wife" for her: It offers an image of art and how artists work (1989, 71). She also tells of a two-year-old girl's reaction to the story. A woman came into a bookstore with the two-year-old and asked the bookseller for a story that could help the child grasp in two-year-old fashion the concept of death. Was there a book that could help release her tears? The bookseller asked for more information. The woman replied that the girl's father had recently shot the girl's mother and himself. The three-year-old son of the bookseller suggested *The Crane Wife.* The woman bought it. Learning of the outcome, the bookseller wrote to Paterson a note of thanks: *The Crane Wife* "helped [to] smooth over the lumps, to open up the tears, to let the child identify with a concept alien to toddlers" (70).

28. Brueggemann claims that such lack of control over reception is a given in all preaching: "No one can any longer imagine that the preaching of the text is heard by members of the community just as it is spoken, or just as it is intended by the preacher. . . . The listening community is engaged in a constructive act of construal, of choosing, discerning and shaping the text through the way the community chooses to listen" (1988, 128).

Notes to Chapter 5.
The Conversation Broadens

1. The sources for these images are as follows: a "discipleship of equals," Elisabeth Schüssler Fiorenza, *In Memory of Her: A Feminist Theological Reconstruction of Christian Origins* (New York: Crossroad, 1984); a "community of friends,"

Sallie McFague, *Models of God: Theology for an Ecological, Nuclear Age* (Philadelphia: Fortress Press, 1987).

2. Similar images of the church as a family or a community of brothers and sisters are found in discussions of church leadership. This literature includes Arthur Merrihew Adams, *Effective Leadership for Today's Church* (Philadelphia: Westminster Press, 1978); Alvin J. Lindgren and Norman Shawchuck, *Let My People Go: Empowering Laity for Ministry* (Nashville: Abingdon Press, 1980); and *A Systems Model of the Church in Ministry and Mission: A General Diagnostic Model for Church Organizational Behavior: Applying a Congruence Perspective* (Chicago: The Center for Parish Development, 1989).

3. Some businesses are rethinking their organizational structures and moving away from hierarchical structures to self-directed teams. See, for example, Marvin R. Weisbord, *Productive Workplaces: Organizing and Managing for Dignity, Meaning, and Community* (San Francisco: Jossey-Bass, 1987); William C. Byham with Jeff Cox, *Zapp!: The Lightning of Empowerment: How to Improve Productivity, Quality and Employee Satisfaction* (Pittsburgh: Development Dimensions International Press, 1989); and James A. Belasco and Ralph C. Stayer, *Flight of the Buffalo: Soaring to Excellence, Learning to Let Employees Lead* (New York: Warner Books, Dove Book, 1993). I am grateful to my brother-in-law, John Robert Day, III, plant manager of the Pfizer Inc. plant, Brooklyn, N.Y., for these references. The central image for the team in *Flight of the Buffalo* is geese flying in formation, working together, not blindly following the herd leader, like buffalo. Browne Barr, in *High Flying Geese: Unexpected Reflections on the Church and Its Ministry* (New York: Seabury Press, 1983), uses this same image for the congregation.

4. Paterson 1989, 72, citing Sumiko Yagawa, *The Crane Wife,* trans. Katherine Paterson (New York: William Morrow, 1981), 25.

5. The continuation of Paterson's discussion of the meaning of "The Crane Wife" suggests that at least for her much of the process of writing fiction is unconscious, with decisions made by the heart rather than by reason. Referring to Yohei, "the rude fellow with a hand on the door," Paterson claims that he also "is myself. . . . I must trust the weaver of thoughts and dreams within and leave her to work as she will. Reason and greed and impatience and curiosity must be kept in check. Else someday I may wake up and find the crane wife has flown away" (1989, 72). Perhaps for some preachers, as well for some fiction writers, the heart not only begins the sermon-making process but also helps make important decisions about content, language, and form along the way.

6. Chopp (1991, 2) acknowledges her indebtedness to Carolyn G. Heilburn (*Writing a Woman's Life* [New York: Ballantine Books, 1988]) for these ideas.

7. In such proclamation, Chopp claims, there is no guarantee of the truth of the testimony because the Word of God always remains open and because proclamation is "always partial" (1991, 99–100).

8. Adams 1981, 28, citing John Cotton, *The True Constitution of a Particular Visible Church Proved by Scripture* (London: n.p., 1642), 6.

Bibliography

Achtemeier, Elizabeth R. 1980. *Creative preaching: Finding the words* (Abingdon Preacher's Library). Edited by William D. Thompson. Nashville: Abingdon Press.

Adams, Doug. 1981. *Meeting house to camp meeting: Toward a history of American free church worship from 1620 to 1835.* Saratoga: Modern Liturgy-Resourse Publications.

Allen, Ronald J. 1983. Shaping sermons by the language of the text. In *Preaching biblically,* edited by Don M. Wardlaw, 29–59. Philadelphia: Westminster Press.

Austin, J. L. 1975. *How to do things with words.* Edited by J. O. Urmson and Marina Sbisà. 2d ed. Cambridge: Harvard University Press.

Barth, Karl. 1963a. *The doctrine of the Word of God: Prolegomena to church dogmatics.* Translated by G. T. Thomson and Harold Knight. Vol. 1:2, *Church dogmatics,* edited by G. W. Bromiley and T. F. Torrance. Edinburgh: T. & T. Clark.

———. 1963b. *The preaching of the Gospel.* Translated by B. E. Hooke. Philadelphia: Westminster Press.

Bartlett, Gene E. 1962. *The audacity of preaching.* New York: Harper & Bros.

Bartow, Charles L. 1980. *The preaching moment: A guide to sermon delivery* (Abingdon Preacher's Library). Edited by William D. Thompson. Nashville: Abingdon Press.

Beardslee, William A. and others. 1989. *Biblical preaching on the death of Jesus.* Nashville: Abingdon Press.

Belenky, Mary Field and others. 1986. *Women's ways of knowing: The development of self, voice, and mind.* Harper Collins, Basic Books.

Best, Ernest. 1988. *From text to sermon: Responsible use of the New Testament in preaching.* 2d ed. Edinburgh: T. & T. Clark.

The Bishops' Committee on Priestly Life and Ministry, National Conference of Catholic Bishops. 1982. *Fulfilled in your hearing: The homily in the Sunday assembly.* Washington, D.C.: Office of Publishing Services, U.S. Catholic Conference.

Bohren, Rudolf. 1965. *Preaching and community.* Translated by David E. Green. Richmond: John Knox Press.

Broadus, John A. 1944. *On the preparation and delivery of sermons.* Revised edition by Jesse Burton Weatherspoon. New York: Harper & Bros.

Brokhoff, John R. 1985. A theology of preaching. In *Heralds to a new age,* edited by Don M. Aycock, 19–29. Elgin, Ill.: Brethren Press.

Brown, H. C., Jr., H. Gordon Clinard, and Jesse J. Northcutt. 1963. *Steps to the sermon: A plan for sermon preparation.* Nashville: Broadman Press.

Brown, Raymond E. 1983. Preaching in the acts of the apostles. In *A new look at preaching,* edited by John Burke, 59–73. Good News Studies, vol. 7. Wilmington, Del.: Michael Glazier.

Browne, Robert E. C. 1958. *The ministry of the Word.* London: SCM Press.

Browning, Don S. 1994. Transcendence and immanence in pastoral care and preaching. In *The treasure of earthen vessels: Explorations in theological anthropology: In honor of James N. Lapsley,* edited by Brian H. Childs and David W. Waanders, 123–36. Louisville: Westminster/John Knox Press.

Brueggemann, Walter. 1988. The social nature of the biblical text for preaching. In *Preaching as a social act: Theology and practice,* edited by Arthur Van Seters, 127–65. Nashville: Abingdon Press.

———. 1989. *Finally comes the poet: Daring speech for proclamation.* Minneapolis: Fortress Press.

Buechner, Frederick. 1977. *Telling the truth: The Gospel as tragedy, comedy, and fairy tale.* San Francisco: Harper & Row.

Burghardt, Walter J. 1983. From study to proclamation. In *A new look at preaching,* edited by John Burke, 25–42. Good News Studies, vol. 7. Wilmington, Del.: Michael Glazier.

Buttrick, David G. 1987. *Homiletic: Moves and structures.* Philadelphia: Fortress Press.

Carroll, Maureen P. 1983. A response. In *Preaching and the non-ordained: An interdisciplinary study,* edited by Nadine Foley, 40–47. Collegeville, Minn.: Liturgical Press.

Chatfield, Donald F. 1984. Textbooks used by teachers of preaching. *Homiletic 9,* no. 2:1–5.

Chopp, Rebecca S. 1991. *The power to speak: Feminism, language, God.* New York: Crossroad.

Clarke, James W. 1960. *Dynamic preaching.* Westwood, N.J.: Fleming H. Revell Co.

Claypool, John. 1980. *The preaching event.* Waco, Tex.: Word Books.

Cleland, James T. 1965. *Preaching to be understood.* Nashville: Abingdon Press.

Cox, James William. 1985. *Preaching.* San Francisco: Harper & Row.

Craddock, Fred B. 1974. *As one without authority: Essays on inductive preaching.* Rev. ed. Enid, Okla.: Phillips University Press.

Crum, Milton, Jr. 1977. *Manual on preaching.* Valley Forge, Pa.: Judson Press.

Daane, James. 1980. *Preaching with confidence: A theological essay on the power of the pulpit.* Grand Rapids: William B. Eerdmans.

Davis, H. Grady. 1958. *Design for preaching.* Philadelphia: Fortress Press.

Dewailly. L.-M. 1964. The silence of the Word. In *The Word: Readings in theology,* compiled at the Canisianum, Innsbruck, 286–97. New York: P. J. Kenedy & Sons.

Dodd, C. H. 1937. *The apostolic preaching and its developments: Three lectures.* With an Introduction by Ernest F. Scott. Chicago: Willett, Clark & Co.

Doyle, Stephen C. 1982. *The Gospel in Word and power: The biblical liturgical homily.* Wilmington, Del.: Michael Glazier.

Duke, Robert W. 1980. *The sermon as God's Word* (Abingdon Preacher's Library). Edited by William D. Thompson. Nashville: Abingdon Press.

Ebeling, Gerhard. 1963. *Word and faith.* Translated by James W. Leitch. London: SCM Press.

Eslinger, Richard L. 1987. *A new hearing: Living options in homiletic methods.* Nashville: Abingdon Press.

Fichtner, Joseph. 1981. *To stand and speak for Christ: A theology of preaching.* New York: Alba House.

Ford, D. W. Cleverley. 1979. *The ministry of the Word.* Grand Rapids: William B. Eerdmans.

Freeman, Harold. 1987. *Variety in biblical preaching: Innovative techniques and fresh forms.* Waco, Tex.: Word Books.

Gilligan, Carol. 1982. *In a different voice: Psychological theory and women's development.* Cambridge: Harvard University Press.

González, Justo L., and Catherine Gunsalus González. 1980. *Liberation preaching: The pulpit and the oppressed* (Abingdon's Preacher's Library). Edited by William D. Thompson. Nashville: Abingdon Press.

Grant, Jacquelyn. 1989. *White women's Christ and Black women's Jesus: Feminist Christology and womanist response* (American Academy of Religion Academy Series). Edited by Susan Thistlethwaite, no. 64. Atlanta: Scholars Press.

Grasso, Domenico. 1964. Kerygma and preaching. In *The Word: Readings in theology,* compiled at the Canisianum, Innsbruck, 220–48. New York: P. J. Kenedy & Sons.

———. 1965. *Proclaiming God's message: A study in the theology of preaching.* Vol. 8, *Liturgical studies.* Notre Dame: University of Notre Dame Press.

Halkes, Catherina. 1980. Feminist theology: An interim assessment. In *Women in a men's church,* edited by Virgil Elizondo and Norbert Greinacher; English language edited by Marcus Lefébure, 110–23. Vol. 134, no. 4, *Concilium: Religion in the eighties.* New York: Seabury Press.

Hall, Thor. 1971. *The future shape of preaching.* Philadelphia: Fortress Press.

Halvorson, Arndt L. 1982. *Authentic preaching.* Minneapolis: Augsburg.

Hill, William J. 1983. What is preaching? One heuristic model from theology. In *A new look at preaching,* edited by John Burke, 113–25. Good News Studies, vol. 7. Wilmington, Del.: Michael Glazier.

Horne, Chevis F. 1983. *Dynamic preaching: How to make your preaching life-changing and powerful.* Nashville: Broadman Press.

Ireson, Gordon W. 1958. *Who shall they hear?* London: SPCK.

Jabusch, Willard Francis. 1980. *The person in the pulpit: Preaching as caring* (Abingdon Preacher's Library). Edited by William D. Thompson. Nashville: Abingdon Press.

Jensen, Richard A. 1980. *Telling the story: Variety and imagination in preaching.* Minneapolis: Augsburg Publishing House.

Keir, Thomas H. 1962. *The Word in worship.* London: Oxford University Press.

Killinger, John. 1969. *The centrality of preaching in the total task of the ministry.* Waco, Tex.: Word Books.

Lewis, Ralph Loren, and Gregg A. Lewis. 1983. *Inductive preaching: Helping people listen.* Westchester, Ill.: Crossway Books, Good News Publishers.

Lischer, Richard. 1981. *A theology of preaching: The dynamics of the Gospel* (Abingdon Preachers Library). Edited by William D. Thompson. Nashville: Abingdon Press.

Long, Thomas G. 1989a. *Preaching and the literary forms of the Bible.* Philadelphia: Fortress Press.

————. 1989b. *The witness of preaching.* Louisville: Westminster/John Knox Press.

Lowry, Eugene L. 1980. *The homiletical plot: The sermon as narrative art form.* Atlanta: John Knox Press.

————. 1985. *Doing time in the pulpit: The relationship between narrative and preaching.* Nashville: Abingdon Press.

————. 1989. *How to preach a parable: Designs for narrative sermons* (Abingdon Preacher's Library). Edited by William D. Thompson. Nashville: Abingdon Press.

————. 1990. The narrative quality of experience as a bridge to preaching. In *Journeys toward narrative preaching,* edited by Wayne Bradley Robinson, 67–77. New York: Pilgrim Press.

Lyotard, Jean-François. 1984. *The postmodern condition: A report on knowledge.* Translated by Geoff Bennington and Brian Massumi. With a Foreword by Fredric Jameson. Vol. 10, *Theory and history of literature,* edited by Wald Godzich and Jochen Schulte-Sasse. Minneapolis: University of Minnesota Press.

Malcomson, William L. 1968. *The preaching event.* Philadelphia: Westminster Press.

Markquart, Edward F. 1985. *Quest for better preaching: Resources for renewal in the pulpit.* Minneapolis: Augsburg Publishing House.

Martell Otero, Loida. 1994. Women doing theology: Una perspectiva evangélica. *Apuntes* 14 (Fall): 75.

McClure, John S. 1995. *The roundtable pulpit: Where leadership and preaching meet.* Nashville: Abingdon Press.

McElvaney, William K. 1989. *Preaching from camelot to covenant: Announcing God's action in the world.* Nashville: Abingdon Press.

McNeil, Jesse Jai. 1961. *The preacher-prophet in mass society.* Grand Rapids: William B. Eerdmans.

McNulty, Frank J. 1985. Introduction: The good eye. In *Preaching better*. Ramsey, N.J.: Paulist Press.

Mitchell, Henry H. 1977. *The recovery of preaching*. New York: Harper & Row.

———. 1979. *Black preaching*. New York: Harper & Row; first published J. P. Lippincott, 1970.

Morris, Colin, 1975. *The Word and the words*. Nashville: Abingdon Press.

Mounce, Robert H. 1960. *The essential nature of New Testament preaching*. Grand Rapids: William B. Eerdmans.

Muehl, William. 1986. *Why preach? Why listen?* Philadelphia: Fortress Press.

Nichols, J. Randall. 1987. *The restoring Word: Preaching as pastoral communication*. San Francisco: Harper & Row.

Paterson, Katherine. 1981. *Gates of excellence: On reading and writing books for children*. New York: Elsevier/Nelson Books.

———. 1989. *The spying heart: More thoughts on reading and writing books for children*. New York: Lodestar Books, E. P. Dutton.

Pearson, Roy Messer. 1954. *The ministry of preaching*. New York: Harper & Bros.

———. 1962. *The preacher: His purpose and practice*. Philadelphia: Westminster Press.

Pittenger, W. Norman. 1962. *Proclaiming Christ today*. Greenwich, Conn.: Seabury Press.

Porteous, Alvin J. 1979. *Preaching to suburban captives*. Valley Forge, Pa.: Judson Press.

Rahner, Karl. 1964. The priesthood: A sermon. In *The Word: Readings in theology*, compiled at the Canisianum, Innsbruck, 249–52. New York: P. J. Kenedy & Sons.

———. 1968. Demythologization and the sermon. Translated by Theodore L. Westow. In *The renewal of preaching: Theory and practice*, edited by Karl Rahner, 20–38. Vol. 33, *Concilium: Theology in the age of renewal: Pastoral theology*. Paramus, N.J.: Paulist Press.

Randolph, David James. 1969. *The renewal of preaching*. Philadelphia: Fortress Press.

Read, David H. C. 1988. *Preaching about the needs of real people* (Preaching About . . . Series). Philadelphia: Westminster Press.

Reid, Clyde H. 1967. *The empty pulpit: A study in preaching as communication*. New York: Harper & Row.

Rhodes, Lynn N. 1987. *Co-creating: A feminist vision of ministry*. Philadelphia: Westminster Press.

Rice, Charles L. 1970. *Interpretation and imagination: The preacher and contemporary literature*. Philadelphia: Fortress Press.

———. 1983. Shaping sermons by the interplay of text and metaphor. In *Preaching biblically*, edited by Don M. Wardlaw, 101–20. Philadelphia: Fortress Press.

Riegert, Eduard R. 1990. *Imaginative shock: Preaching and metaphor.* Burlington, Ont.: Trinity Press.

Ritschl, Dietrich. 1960. *A theology of proclamation.* Richmond: John Knox Press.

Russell, Letty M. 1993. *Church in the round: Feminist interpretation of the church.* Louisville: Westminster/John Knox Press.

Salmon, Bruce C. 1988. *Storytelling in preaching: A guide to the theory and practice.* Nashville: Broadman Press.

Scherer, Paul. 1965. *The word God sent.* New York: Harper & Row.

Schillebeeckx, Edward. 1964. Revelation in word and deed. In *The Word: Readings in theology,* compiled at the Canisianum, Innsbruck, 255–72. New York: P. J. Kenedy & Sons.

Schmaus, Michael. 1966. *Preaching as a saving encounter.* Translated by J. Holland Smith. Staten Island, N.Y.: St. Paul, Alba House.

Schüssler Fiorenza, Elisabeth. 1983. Response. In *A new look at preaching,* edited by John Burke, 43–55. Good News Studies, vol. 7. Wilmington, Del.: Michael Glazier.

Scott, Bernard Brandon. 1985. *The Word of God in words: Reading and preaching* (Fortress Resources for Preaching). Philadelphia: Fortress Press.

Semmelroth, Otto. 1965. *The preaching Word: On the theology of proclamation.* Translated by John Jay Hughes. New York: Herder & Herder.

Sider, Ronald J., and Michael A. King. 1987. *Preaching about life in a threatening world* (Preaching About . . . Series). Philadelphia: Westminster Press.

Sittler, Joseph. 1966. *The anguish of preaching.* Philadelphia: Fortress Press.

Sleeth, Ronald E. 1964. *Proclaiming the Word.* Nashville: Abingdon Press.

———. 1986. *God's Word and our words: Basic homiletics.* With a Foreword by Thomas G. Long. Atlanta: John Knox Press.

Smith, Christine M. 1989. *Weaving the sermon: Preaching in a feminist perspective.* Louisville: Westminster/John Knox Press.

Swank, George W. 1981. *Dialogic style in preaching.* Valley Forge, Pa.: Judson Press.

Taylor, Gardner. 1983. Shaping sermons by the shape of text and preacher. In *Preaching biblically,* edited by Don M. Wardlaw, 137–52. Philadelphia: Westminster Press.

Thielicke, Helmut. 1965. *The trouble with the church.* Edited and translated by John W. Doberstein. New York: Harper & Row.

Thompson, Claude H. 1962. *Theology of the kerygma: A study in primitive preaching.* Englewood Cliffs, N.J.: Prentice-Hall.

Thompson, William D. 1981. *Preaching biblically: Exegesis and interpretation* (Abingdon Preacher's Library). Edited by William D. Thompson. Nashville: Abingdon Press.

Thulin, Richard L. 1990. Retelling biblical narratives as the foundation for preaching. In *Journeys toward narrative preaching,* edited by Wayne Bradley Robinson, 7–18. New York: Pilgrim Press.

Tizard, Leslie James. 1958. *Preaching: The act of communication.* New York: Oxford University Press.

Tostengard, Sheldon A. 1989. *The spoken Word* (Fortress Resources for Preaching). Philadelphia: Fortress Press.

Tracy, David. 1987. *Plurality and ambiguity: Hermeneutics, religion, hope.* San Francisco: Harper & Row.

Troeger, Thomas H. 1982. *Creating fresh images for preaching: New rungs for Jacob's ladder* (More Effective Preaching Series). Valley Forge, Pa.: Judson Press.

————. 1983. Shaping sermons by the encounter of text with preacher. In *Preaching biblically,* edited by Don. M. Wardlaw, 153–73. Philadelphia: Westminster Press.

von Allmen, Jean-Jacques. 1962. *Preaching and congregation.* Translated by B. L. Nicholas. Ecumenical Studies in Worship, no. 10. Richmond: John Knox Press.

Ward, Ronald A. 1958. *Royal sacrament: The preacher and his message.* London: Marshall, Morgan & Scott.

Wardlaw, Don M. 1983. Introduction: The need for new shapes. In *Preaching biblically,* edited by Don M. Wardlaw, 11–25. Philadelphia: Westminster Press.

Wardlaw, Don M., ed. 1989. *Learning preaching: Understanding and participating in the process.* Lincoln, Ill.: The Academy of Homiletics, Lincoln Christian College and Seminary Press.

Welsh, Clement. 1974. *Preaching in a new key: Studies in the psychology of thinking and listening.* Philadelphia: United Church Press, Pilgrim Press.

West, Robin. 1988. Jurisprudence and gender. *The University of Chicago Law Review* 55 (Winter):1–72.

White, Hugh C. 1988. Introduction: Speech act theory and literary criticism. *Semeia: An Experimental Journal for Biblical Criticism* 41:1–24.

Wilson, Paul S. 1988. *Imagination of the heart: New understandings in preaching.* Nashville: Abingdon Press.

Wilson-Kastner, Patricia. 1989. *Imagery for preaching.* Minneapolis: Fortress Press.

Wright, James. 1958. *A preacher's questionnaire.* Edinburgh: St. Andrew's Press.

Young, Robert D. 1979. *Religious imagination: God's gift to prophets and preachers.* Philadelphia: Westminster Press.

Index of Authors

Index of Subjects